NANCY WYNNE-JONES

Nancy Wynne-Jones

— AT EIGHTY —

BRIAN FALLON

GANDON EDITIONS

NANCY WYNNE-JONES AT EIGHTY
by Brian Fallon

Published by Gandon Editions on the occasion of the
artist's 80th birthday.

© Gandon Editions and the artist, 2002.
All rights reserved.

ISBN 0946846 375

Design	John O'Regan
	(© Gandon Editions, 2002)
Production	Nicola Dearey, Gandon
Photography	Gillian Buckley (art works)
	Bob Berry (Co Wicklow)
Printing	Nicholson & Bass, Belfast
Distribution	Gandon Distribution, Kinsale

GANDON EDITIONS
Oysterhaven, Kinsale, Co Cork, Ireland
tel: +353 (0)21-4770830 / fax: 021-4770755
e-mail: gandon@eircom.net
www.gandon-editions.com

front cover	*Pale Bog*
	2001, acrylic on canvas, 76 x 102 cm
	(30 x 40 in), detail [see page 170]
frontispiece	*Pond in October*
	1990-91, acrylic on canvas, 91.5 x 122 cm
	(36 x 48 in), detail [see page 128]
title page	*Self-Portrait*
	1953, oil on board, 46 x 30.5 cm (18 x 12 in)
endpapers	views of the artist's home in Co Wicklow

Acknowledgements and thanks to
Pat and John Taylor, Taylor Galleries, Dublin

Gandon Editions is grant-aided by The Arts Council /
An Chomhairle Ealaíon

Contents

Nancy Wynne-Jones:
"Ulysses ... Possess these shores with me"

INTRODUCTION BY HILARY PYLE

Landscape is both terrene and mirage. The reality of what one sees, which is solid and tangible, has been rearranged by effects of light, distance and weather, and transformed into something ephemeral. According to Simon Scharma, what is seen by the viewer is a work of the mind, with unconnected permutations of the viewing experience, such as 'strata' of memory, colluding with the layers of rock in a determination to deceive the eye. Some commentators go further, regarding landscape as a purely aesthetic notion, enhanced through the response of painters, poets and musicians to the subtleties of the illusion. Artists have certainly influenced ways of looking by means of magical descriptions of what they themselves have seen. For the writer Henri Frederic Amiel, any landscape is '*un etat de l'ame*' – a condition of the soul.

When the term 'landscape' was invented by the Netherlandish painters who originally introduced non-figurative panoramic scenes as a new kind of painting, the word carried with it a nuance of human power, for the 'skip' in 'landskip', as it then was, implied to 'create' or 'ordain' – perhaps as in 'lordship'. Despite their reputation for fidelity in representation, these first landscapists of the humanist 17th century were declaring their intention to manipulate and to make what they saw their own.

Nancy Wynne-Jones is well aware of the complexity of the reality and the illusion. Ancient geological contours, variously clothed by nature in different ages or by man's manoeuvrings, instantly attract her – water free on its own level or coaxed to float within the limits of contrived cradles, phenomenal trees, crafted turf stacks making small sculptural statements in the loose hugeness of the swelling bog, air assuming unexpected colours. Roads, especially in her painting, are like pilgrims hastening on their way into the unknown. She too wants to 'possess' the land her eye chooses, not necessarily to reshape or 'ordain' it, but – as a lover rushing into the arms of her beloved – to share and understand the huge, mystic, universal emotions.

She has always lived in and on the land, in Wales, Cornwall and Ireland, and throughout her life has sketched the scenes and vistas through which she has passed. Environments have made deep

Corvoley, 2001 / opposite: *Across to Achill*, 2000 (detail, see page 167)

and different impressions on her, and her early sketches (worked with watercolour sticks for their freedom) have a thrilling spontaneity, and in their economical observation and skilful handling of colour, anticipate her mature work. All the same, it was some time before she recognised the importance of this intuitive sketching. She didn't find her artistic way easily. Starting out on her career as an artist, her initial instinct was to avoid what had become a conventional subject, and to forge an abstract and innovative style for herself. Indeed she will say that the only thing she was sure about for many years was that she must paint. Searching for a personal style and subject matter was a lengthy process, but the striving, which is an essential element of lasting art, brought with it the unforgettable and splendid experiences which she describes in this book.

The first step in the journey was separating the theoretical and the academic – which intrigue her incessantly – from the intellectual and the instinctive that are her strength. Peter Lanyon in Cornwall was the cornerstone of those early efforts to find an individual style, and she found the company of the artistic community in St Ives rare and stimulating. Abstract Expressionism was the international mode of the day, and Lanyon encouraged her to make her oil painting broad and gestural. She is naturally spontaneous, and was a little impatient with his meticulous preliminaries, but she did modify the colour that was innate in her to match his sparse black and white, and, adopting a sweeping pitch guided by the geometric forms in her environment, painted abstracts that found identities as portraits of her friends or as characters in the *Odyssey* or in Celtic epic. The thrust in these paintings is generally vertical, grandly formal, relating to the bulk and sheer profile of the cliffs around her, while the tentative symbolism reflects a deep love of ancient classical legend.

She continued over the years experimenting with technique, turning to spray painting, which created new molecular surfaces, still smooth and flat, economic in colour, but strongly composed and moodily expressive. Circumstances always provided a challenge, and gave her the opportunity to practise in egg tempera, and in acrylic in its early days, which she has returned to now as her main medium.

In the early 1970s, book-knowledge led her to an encounter with Persian tiles (albeit reproduced in black and white), which opened up a brighter phase, with Cubist effects in her still life paintings of flowers and musical instruments. The contrast of these works with her St Ives paintings is dramatic, the colour the more intense no doubt after years of suppressing it. Colour was proving to be the most important thing, and was instinctive to her, like her talent for composition, which became apparent when she was a girl in music, and then renewed itself in her structural sense when working in paint. From the beginning, music and painting, together with her poetic insight, were shaping her artistic personality.

Nancy Wynne-Jones reckons that she was 52 when she was finally finished with her theoretical wanderings and realised that the freedom of expression she had always been seeking was already within her, with 'landscape' as her subject. It was roughly the same time as she took up composing again, creating 'landscapes' for orchestra. The land was in her blood, but while she loved the countrysides of Wales and Cornwall, and the quieter scenery of Cork, cultivated for centuries (where she moved not long after her marriage to sculptor Conor Fallon), it was the wildness of western Ireland that ultimately captivated her. She discovered Mayo, a country waiting to be imagined in a postmodern world, and, in the creating, Mayo discovered her true self.

Her method in this powerful painting is the same as when she started sketching in the 1950s, though she now uses oil pastels, with their bold vibrancy, in these outdoor sketches of strong van Gogh-like line. These translate into acrylic in the studio – not as replicas, but as large melodic variations with alternating intonations of place and mood. The paint is applied now in layers with glazes, creating a rich, pulsing, sensual surface, delicately controlled within the new freedom. She invites the landscape into herself by way of the sketches. The landscape she paints out later is transformed, manifestly figureless, but imbued with human emotion and presence in all its wild energy. The tension is that of an acrobat striding out confidently on a well-tried tightrope. The light captures the underlying elation; the diagonal urgency which supplants the vertical thrust of her first classical abstracts is echoed in any surface marks, which lends these larger compositions the immediacy of her oil pastel drawings.

In some respects, coming into her own happened at an unlikely time. On 3 August of this year, in the *Irish Times*, Aidan Dunne reiterated, with a touch of sarcasm, an idea that is prevalent: 'Painting is unfashionable. The most extreme view is that in the brave, new, post-modern world of installation and photography, video and other more nebulous activities, painting is an anachronism, that there is no longer any painting, only 'painting' – it has been relocated, to borrow a phrase from Denis Donoghue, between the irony of inverted commas.' However, during a second Irish renaissance when women artists are in their element, in company with a surprising number of other original artists Nancy Wynne-Jones has demonstrated that although 'landscape' may be more properly located between inverted commas, 'painting' is still very much alive, and burgeoning with imagination. She may have taken the long route in her youth, but 'landscape' was always at the centre of the road – the invisible source of her St Ives portraits, the animation in the background of her Cork still lifes.

One totally different experience has been the landscape in Africa, where the natural intensity of colour bowled her over. The acrylics that came out of it, shown in Dublin in 2000, exude warmth, brooding atmosphere, the teeming growth of the tropics. The last exhibitions of the old century show her almost drunk with the landscape mode, paint flowing from her broad brush at a lyrical pitch.

She named her most recent exhibition *I sing thy praise, Mayo*. These latest canvases and works on paper sing unreservedly, conveying the joyousness of the air stroking her face and hands at the same time as it brushes the edges of mountain and lake. As Elgar has said, 'Music is in the air, you simply take as much of it as you want.' Air is now the subject of her paintings, dancing in the space between the artist and the distant view, locating the foreground, its physicality indicated in light, unobtrusive, diagonal strokes, an extra presence. In it she finds a visual third dimension, the nearest she can come to representing the true reality of the scene which is illusion. Truly she has 'possessed' this landscape, just as this landscape has possessed her.

HILARY PYLE is a writer and critic, and Yeats Curator at the National Gallery of Ireland. She has written many books, including *James Stephens: his work and an account of his life* (RKP, 1965); *Jack B Yeats: a biography* (RKP, 1970; reprinted 1989); *The Different Worlds of Jack B Yeats* (Irish Academic Press, 1994); and *Yeats – Portrait of an Artistic Family* (Merrell Holberton, 1997).

A Subtle Poet of the Palette

ESSAY BY BRIAN FALLON

Perhaps I can allow myself a little personal reminiscence to begin with. Nancy Wynne-Jones is, of course, my sister-in-law, but I had known and esteemed her for several years before she married my sculptor-brother, Conor, in 1966. I first met her in St Ives in, I think, the late summer or early autumn of 1961, while on a visit to my old friend Tony O'Malley who had settled there the previous year. Through her I first met Peter Lanyon, an encounter I remember vividly, though I was suffering from the aftermath of a smallpox inoculation (there was an epidemic in Wales, through which I had come) and was incapable of saying much. I also, on that visit and a number of subsequent ones, met Bryan Wynter, Roger Hilton, Patrick Heron, Alan Lowndes and Breon O'Casey, among others. St Ives fairly swarmed with artists, true and false. John Wells, Denis Mitchell, Patrick Hayman and Terry Frost I did not get to know until much later.

Nancy then lived in the Battery, which presumably had at one stage been exactly what its name indicated, and probably was built during the national scare of a Napoleonic invasion. It stood – and still stands, to my knowledge – slightly apart from St Ives itself, on a patch of green-turfed high ground in the area known as the Island, overlooking the Atlantic. We had some wild (though not orgiastic) evenings there, and I remember one in particular, when Nancy played records of Indian ragas and some of the guests danced ecstatically in a pseudo-Indian style. And, a little later, I remember gay days and nights in Trevaylor, the old Cornish manor house she moved to, close to the village of Gulval a few miles outside Penzance.

Those were days that live on in the memory, and the camaraderie and sense of creative fellowship in St Ives was something I had never encountered before. It seems to me that the large exhibition *St Ives 1939-1964*, which was mounted at the Tate Gallery in London in 1985, somehow failed almost entirely to convey or recapture the essential gusto and fun and artistic solidarity which pervaded that small area of the Land's End peninsula. There was rather too much post-Nicholson pastiche, too much of the spidery, attenuated kind of abstract art which was a blight on British art a generation ago; in short, too much formalism and Modernist academicism. Was this rather thin-

Pond with Orange Tree and Little House, 1997 / opposite: *Blue Coast*, 1958 (detail, see page 53)

blooded and purist art really the essence of the vital, humorous, often opinionated men and women of the milieu I saw and knew at first hand, however briefly and peripherally? Not, in my own opinion, by several Cornish sea-miles. Instead, it was the St Ives School suitably watered down and homogenised for academics and writers of theses, who could expand smugly on the legacy of Gabo, Nicholson and Hepworth, and reduce it all to stock art-historical terminology. Almost everything that was personal, regional, fresh, uninhibited, had been subtly smoothed away by the emery-paper of commentators and analysts. An uninformed visitor might easily have carried away the final impression that (apart from Alfred Wallis) St Ives art consisted of Nicholson and Hepworth and their immediate followers, and not a great deal else. Of course Lanyon, Frost, Heron, Hilton and other leading figures were represented, yet somehow they looked devitalised and shrunken in this art-museum context. And admirable painters such as John Tunnard, Patrick Hayman and Alan Lowndes seem to have been included almost as an afterthought.[1] Nancy herself was not represented, although she had been included in various prestige group shows of Cornish art, had created some of the subtlest delineations of the local landscape, and had also painted striking portraits of artist-colleagues, including Lanyon, Hilton and O'Malley. There has been sporadic talk since then of another major St Ives exhibition. If that ever happens then let us hope it is less myopic in its viewpoint, and far more catholic in its choices.

It seems generally agreed that there is something called St Ives style, but it cannot be blue-printed, nor can it be pinned down adequately through a few rather easy generalisations about form and colour.[2] The style is and was the men and the women who created it. I do not claim for a moment to be a close historian of those years – far from it, in fact. What I do believe is that creative activity revolved around the irradiating personalities of a small handful of people, most of whom had radically differing outlooks, styles and mentalities. Art history would seem to prove that 'schools' are created as much by mutual antagonisms and incompatibility between key individuals (e.g. Manet and Degas) as they are by common aims or ideals. More often than not, it is either the contemporary journalists or slightly later historians – *laudatores temporis acti* – who manufacture the cloak of a group identity. In short, St Ives art was much more varied, not to say much more interesting, than its textbook image suggests.

But perhaps I have gone on too much about that particular point or angle, and certainly Nancy herself harbours no regrets about it, though I should say that nobody enjoyed that time and milieu more thoroughly than she did. I have heard her say on a number of occasions that when she arrived there first in 1957, the aura of creativity in that small Cornish fishing town was almost palpable, and like nothing she has experienced since. Today that aura has vanished. I have visited St Ives a number of times in the past two decades, and I found it almost a ghost town compared with the magical place I remembered. There may still be talented people active there, but broadly speaking history has left it behind, just as it has left behind Concarneau, Pont-Aven, Grez-sur-Loing, Worpswede, or any other locale which was once a nerve centre of creativity. When, about a dozen years ago, Tony and Jane O'Malley gave up their studio overlooking Porthmeor Beach and moved to Ireland, they were tacitly acknowledging the fact that the old St Ives was gone, and probably for good. Only in Newlyn did some of the old creativity linger on.

It is stating the obvious to say that Cornwall had a major influence on Nancy's art, but I would not, myself, ultimately class her as belonging to the St Ives School in the sense that Frost, Heron, etc, belonged to it. In any case, her work of the past three decades has largely distanced her from Cornish abstraction, and even from much of her own earlier work as well, though of course a large residue remains. Where then to place her, and in what context? She does, in certain respects, resemble the American Painterly Realists of a few decades ago, who learned both from abstraction and from the Bonnard-Vuillard tradition. However, I would not press the similarity too far.[3]

Sometimes I think of a parallel with Winifred Nicholson, but Nicholson's mentality was utterly and exclusively English, even in her type of nature lyricism, while Nancy is at once more Celtic and more Continental. Tony O'Malley was, like Nancy, an outsider in Cornwall who has since settled in Ireland, but their differences seem more obvious than their common qualities. Ireland has some excellent painters who work in areas not dissimilar from hers, notably Seán McSweeney, Basil Blackshaw, Camille Souter, and one or two more, but she is not really like any of them. One thing she has, however, is a sensibility which is recognisably Celtic, and I make no apology for using a term which seemingly has lost currency and even respect. If I knew a better and more precise word for this quality I would gladly employ it, but I know of none, and surely it is as legitimate a phrase as Teutonic, Latin, Nordic, etc.

All this is probably not so much a question of style, in the end, as of sensibility. The type of lyrical awareness which informs her work is common to Dylan Thomas, Lanyon, perhaps David Jones, as well as to much of Jack Yeats and Patrick Collins, though there are also flashes of it in that other ultra-English painter, Ivon Hitchens. I know and recognise this quality but cannot define it, though I might say, very tentatively, that it comes close to a pantheistic earth sense while remaining unfettered and almost ethereal. It is quite free of the gentility and inhibiting good taste which infected as potentially gifted a painter as Gwen John, who, ironically, was Welsh by blood and background but never quite managed to throw off the devitalising legacy of her London art training. In spite of her long domicile in France, her tonal 'refinement' ultimately drained the blood from her work, leaving it chalky and pallid, whereas Nancy, who has never lived for any long period on the Continent, has a natural affinity with its art, and at times handles colour like a Frenchwoman born. She is equally at home with Italian Renaissance art as with contemporary trends, and might even say, like the musician Cecil Gray (a Scot), that she is 'both Celt and Latin'.[4]

She is Welsh by birth and background, English and Cornish by training, and has since become virtually a naturalised Irish painter. Her development has been idiosyncratic, and as an artist she is an individualist – what the French would call an independent – who is fully aware of recent developments but sticks to her own style and vision. Her recent exhibitions have given a slightly simplified view of her as essentially a landscapist, and it is true that landscape has dominated her output, but her range is much wider and embraces still life, portraits, interiors with and without figures, straightforward figurative works, even animal subjects. Though she has always drawn fluently and quite realistically from nature, abstraction dominated her work for decades, and plainly she has carried over the disciplines of abstract art into her later work. She never entirely abandoned it, in fact, and her recent landscapes often incorporate elements from Abstract Expressionism, including its gestural brushwork and broad simplifications, so in effect she makes her own, highly original synthesis of depiction and abstraction.

In any case, the old divide between abstraction and realism no longer makes much sense, since most good figurative painters have absorbed the lessons of abstract art, while abstractionists such as Ellsworth Kelly frequently begin with motifs drawn or observed from nature and everyday reality. There is no creative schizophrenia involved, and Nancy's works in any style, while superficially they may seem different from one another, are patently in the same handwriting and painted with the same touch.

Nancy herself says she is, at heart, an Abstract Expressionist. That may sound a little odd when you consider that so much of her work is dominated by landscape, or at least landscape themes, and that she has painted still life, portraits, etc, as already mentioned. It does in fact suggest an artist who, a generation ago, felt the abstract currents of the time, when these were still relatively avant-garde, but who has since lapsed into a more traditional approach. Yet even a quick glance at her output over decades will show that while the outward manner may vary, its essential syntax has not altered; her basic shapes, brushwork and marks remain relatively unchanged, whatever the mutations of style. And above all, the basis of her art, whether abstract or figurative, has always been in nature in the broadest sense. This is, I believe, inherent in Abstract Expressionism itself. It is a style built largely on natural rhythms, organic shapes, metamorphosis, growth and decay.

This may sound a sweeping claim, and already I can hear angry mutterings about the New York School and its metropolitan dynamism, in particular. But was American abstraction so essentially urban a phenomenon as is claimed? Commentators have traced the genesis of Franz Kline's black-and-white canvases to memories of the Pennsylvanian landscape, both rural and industrialised; de Kooning's late works often refer to seascapes he saw from his Long Island home; Pollock's paintings have a definite mythic-nature element, and were also influenced by Indian pictographs in sand. The urban supremacy in American art did not really begin until the Pop movement, which by its very nature was a big-city affair – you cannot easily envisage Warhol setting up an easel in the middle of a field or forest. By contrast, Abstract Expressionism drew heavily on the organic-metamorphic aspect of Surrealism, particularly as represented by André Masson, and both movements belong mainly to the Romantic side of the spectrum.[6] Its polar opposite was Minimalism, which ignored most 'natural' forms in favour of simple, reiterated geometric shapes and architectural motifs. (It is a suggestive fact that a number of prominent Minimalists were architects by training.) Broadly speaking, it rejected 'nature' as almost a foreign body, and like many of the Bauhaus and Constructivist artists before it, laid stress on an urban and industrial environment shaped by man.

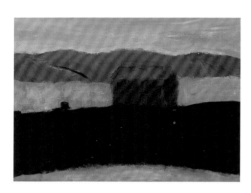

Red Vineyard, 1989

I do not for a moment suggest that all Constructivist or 'formalist' art is inherently anti-nature, or that it is per se any less 'expressive' than Expressionism, whether abstract or figurative. In practice, both these streams of Modernism have fertilised each other and have often fought under the same banner. The fact remains that in their purest forms, they are radically different from each other and have a different ancestry and even a different aesthetic. You cannot, for instance, turn a Mondrian into a Soutine, a Malevich into a Chagall, or a Sol LeWitt into a Lucien Freud. In her earliest phase Nancy painted some abstract pictures based on squares (these I have never seen), but the type of abstraction she followed in her early St Ives years was free and lyrical, as suited her style and temperament. To a great extent it was formed under the tutelage of Peter Lanyon, whose pupil and/or follower she was at the time. Lanyon was, among other things, an inspiring teacher, and not only in the technical sense. Nancy did not work under him as a beginner or tyro. She was an 'advanced' pupil, and was not there to learn the rudiments of painting and drawing (she was always, in fact, an excellent draughtswoman). What Lanyon taught was mainly his own approach to landscape, which involved experiencing it from many angles and viewpoints. He even encouraged his pupils to lie on their backs in the open in order to get away from the conventional concepts of foreground and background, fixed perspectives, sky and horizon.

In Lanyon's mature work, land, sky and sea are presented as a simultaneous sensation, and the viewer is 'in' the painting as a participant, rather than as a spectator viewing it from a certain distance or vantage. Of course, this has its roots in the multiple perspectives of Cubism, but it also relates to modern 'existential' consciousness. (This may sound terribly pretentious, I realise, but then art-critical terminology has not yet quite managed to invent the right words for such things.) Lanyon, in the finest of his Cornish paintings, not only brought in landscape configuration, the air, light, sea and weather, he added extra layers of meaning from the past and its multiple associations. This was a very taxing programme, liable to trip up even major talents such as he, so it is no wonder that Lanyon's work is not always fully realised, or that his pictures lack coherence at times. Allowing for all that, and for the fact that he died while still in his middle forties, he was an astonishing innovator who, above all, showed that the most advanced abstract style could be used to express the spirit of place, and that, conversely, the particular could be used to suggest the general. There were other excellent painters in St Ives, but he remains the most original, and his special synthesis – which derived as much from the example of Naum Gabo's Constructivist sculpture as it did from the Romantic landscape tradition, from Constable to Hitchens – is as relevant today as it was forty years ago.[7]

The more purist, geometric aspect of St Ives art stems mainly from Ben Nicholson, whose real genius was probably for eclecticism in the very best sense. He managed to reconcile Braque with Mondrian, landscape sensibility with architectonic rigour, and an essential Englishness with various Continental trends, including Cubism. In retrospect, it was rather a misfortune that many artists of a younger generation saw him as a departure to be followed creatively, whereas he was

The Window, 1982

really more of a terminal point. Nicholson was not, at heart, a radical innovator, though no doubt much could be learned from him, and a great deal was, in fact, particularly in the technical sense. He had the peculiarly English talent for the *via media* and for establishing a balance between opposites. That, after all, appears to have been the great secret of English statesmanship over centuries – to maintain an equilibrium between often hostile forces, the so-called balance of power. His many imitators were for the most part mere academics of the Modern movement, taking his hard-won synthesis to a stage where it became bloodless and patently derivative. Lanyon, by comparison, a man of a different generation from Nicholson and Hepworth, looked to the future, and arguably died before he had fully said his say. He too had his valid followers and vapid imitators, but his work was genuinely open-ended and revealed new vistas, whereas Nicholson for the most part presented an elegant closed door.

In the immediate years before she moved to Ireland, Nancy appears to have struck out in a number of directions, and though the result was almost always characterful and interesting, she now feels that the output of those years was, in the main, away from her true development. In her own words: 'The years between 1965 and our leaving Cornwall in 1972 were years of uncertainty for me in my work. I attempted various paths – mythologies, airbrush abstracts, still lifes. I suppose they were attempts to develop from Abstract Expressionism. All seemed to me to be wrong decisions and were quickly discontinued, although some were exhibited.'[8] She and her husband left for a number of reasons – the growing commercialism of Cornwall for mass tourism, the shift away from it as a creative centre (which had begun with Lanyon's death), the encroachments of the drug culture along with a rootless fringe bohemianism, and the wish to bring up their children in Ireland. So they settled in Kinsale, which they found a sympathetic and unspoiled place in which to work (Conor Fallon, who had begun as a painter, was now fully committed to sculpture.) In her own words again: 'The distance from Dublin left us rather isolated, and both Conor and I benefited at this time from being able to work away from the critical eyes of other artists.'

The airbrush pictures mentioned were painted with a spray-gun, and were on a fairly large scale, at least for her. They were executed with great brio and immediacy, since the method itself is rapid and almost improvisatory, though I understand that it also needs real skill and quickness of decision. However, in spite of the occasional brilliance of the effects obtained, Nancy herself seems to have tired of the medium, feeling that some dimension or other was missing. She was usually happy to try new themes and break new ground, but if she once became convinced that she had strayed too far from the tonic key of her development, she was correspondingly quick to write off the result as a dead end. I have known her to repaint, or, on occasions, even to destroy pictures which I considered wholly successful but which she herself felt did not correspond exactly to the conception at the back of her mind. I do not believe, by the way, that artists are necessarily their own best critics. Yet in the end, they can be the only true assessors of how adequately they have translated the picture they carry in their heads into the picture they see before them on the easel or on the wall. I have found Nancy to be quite ruthless in this regard, and all her work must past this inner censor before it is let out.

In the middle and late 1960s she painted a number of smallish, lyrically direct works in tempera, which, in retrospect, foreshadowed many elements of her recent painting. One in particular I have been familiar with for years is *Summer Road* (1965), which looks forward to many of the landscapes she painted in Ireland (I well remember it hanging on a wall in Trevaylor.) It suggests a view from a car travelling at speed, while the summer hedgerows go by in a warm blur. The road is a thrusting yellow shape, and the underlying composition seems to show some of the spiral method or motif which Lanyon used so often.[9]

After she and her husband moved to Kinsale, she gradually came to terms with the Cork landscape, and painted more consistently and more evenly in quality than she had done for years, or perhaps had ever done. A late developer in some respects, she was finally coming wholly into her own. Since many of these landscapes are small in format, I am still struck by their sense of space and distance, and also by their uncompromising quality, by which I do not mean any hardness or edginess of style. They simplify without distortion or mannerism, and catch the spirit of a specific place without getting bogged down in the minutiae of detail or in overmuch local colour. I well remember one accomplished Irish landscape painter almost recoiling from these works and saying that they were 'too green' – exactly the kind of reaction which Constable had to cope with in his day, and which in itself says much about the blinkers of convention with which even seasoned, observant painters approach their native countryside and its tones. That fierce, sappy green is of course an essential colour in our landscape, and is an aspect of it which has immediately impressed itself upon visitors. But she is equally adept at rendering the peculiar rusty tones of autumn, and a certain cold, wet light which I associate with early spring.

She also, around this time, produced some memorable images of the estuary lands on the Cork coast, and of Kinsale harbour, which she could see just below her studio. However, she had probably exhausted the motifs of the local landscape by the time she moved to Wicklow at the end of the 1980s, and the wooded, hilly country in which she now lives has given her a new range of ideas, and has extended the resources of an already rich, subtle palette. Her colour sense, by the way, is very much her own, and is quite distinct from that of the better-known St Ives painters, who tended (though Heron and Wynter were exceptions) to anchor their palette rather low in the scale. In this area she even seems near to the spirit of French art, and generally handles 'high' colour with a brio unusual in British-trained painters, who tend traditionally to be tonalists rather than colourists. She is also original in her use of close, rather ochreous tones. It is worth recalling that she has always been an avid traveller, especially to southern regions, and has visited Italy and Crete and (several times) southern France, while more recently she added a whole dimension to her vision and palette with a stay in South Africa. Even the most torrid light of these regions does not seem to have posed her any more intractable problems than the moisture-laden light of southern Ireland or the Mayo bogs. Nancy also renders water with great sensitivity, although she has rarely painted the sea. The pond in front of her Wicklow home, in particular, and the trees and plants around it have been painted in various seasons of the year and with all possible tonal contrasts. Comparison seems unavoidable here with Seán McSweeney's pictorial variations of his patch of bog near the Sligo coastline, or with Tony O'Malley's paintings of his own garden pool at Callan, or even – to bring in the prototype of it all – with Monet.[10]

I believe Nancy to be a considerable painter, who cannot be slotted into any school or grouping known to me, but stands more or less alone. I am far from being alone in estimating her highly. Various shrewd judges side with me, and their number is growing steadily as her style gains currency among the art-loving public. The mini-retrospective of her work which opened in University College Cork in 1992, travelling on to Galway, Limerick, Letterkenny, and finally Dublin, was a gallant enterprise in itself, but too limited in scope to take her full measure.[11] Besides, much has happened in her art since then, including her discovery of the Mayo bogs and the very productive South African interlude. A large exhibition, carefully and knowledgeably chosen, but also inclusive and broad in its choice, is now overdue to represent her considerable output over half a century.

The richness and variety of her paintings, however, should not be allowed to overshadow wholly her (very large) output of pastels and black-and-white drawings, which maintain a level that compares with any of her contemporaries in whatever country. Throughout her various shifts in style as a painter, this aspect of her work seems to have remained constant, and while I can see the legacy of Lanyon over a certain period, many or most of her drawings are without a whiff of his influence – or indeed anybody else's – but are wholly her own. I would dearly like to see a major exhibition mounted of these, though there must be a daunting body of work to choose from. Apart from their sheer quality, they would underline the fact that there is a wiry armature – or musculature – of form beneath the surface freedom and informality of so many of the paintings, and that her apparent spontaneity is guided by a shrewd, vastly experienced hand and brain.

BRIAN FALLON was born in Cootehill, Co Cavan, in 1933, and was educated at Trinity College Dublin. He was art critic with the *Irish Times* for 35 years, and was also literary editor from 1977 to 1988. He is the author of *Irish Art 1830-1990*, and *An Age of Innocence*, a history of Irish culture from 1930 to 1960, as well as various monographs. He has edited the collected poems of his father, Padraic Fallon, for Carcanet Press.

ENDNOTES

An earlier version of this essay appeared in the catalogue
Nancy Wynne-Jones – Retrospective Exhibition (Visual
Arts Committee, UCC, Cork, 1992)

[1] This tendency was taken to extreme limits in the large
and much-publicised exhibition of 20th-century
British art at the Royal Academy in London in 1987.
Critical good sense seemed more or less to vanish
under art-historical premises, and major artists such
as John Tunnard and John Wells were wholly ignored,
among others. See Susan Compton (ed), *British Art in
the 20th Century: the Modern Movement* (Prestel-
Verlag, Munich & New York, 1987).

[2] The art historian Margaret Garlake has described St
Ives style as 'perceptual abstraction'. See her book
New Art New World: British Art in Postwar Society
(Yale University Press, London and New Haven,
1998).

[3] The so-called Painterly Realists represent a chapter in
American art which is still little known in Europe.
Their leading figure was Fairfield Porter (1907-1975).
Artists such as Jane Freilicher were also associated
with it.

[4] See his remarkable autobiography *Musical Chairs*
(London, 1948) which has since been reprinted as a
paperback

[5] See Stravinsky's *Conversations with Robert Craft*,
reprinted many times by Penguin Books.

[6] The importance of Masson as a link between
European Surrealism and American 'action painting'
has been stressed by the late Herbert Read, among
others. Jackson Pollock, in particular, seems to have
owed him a considerable debt.

[7] See *Peter Lanyon 1918-1964* by the artist's son,
Andrew Lanyon (published by the author, Newlyn,
Penzance, 1991).

[8] Quoted from the catalogue of her 1992 retrospective
(see above).

[9] I suspect that the originator of this – apart from
Gabo – was Ivon Hitchens, whose innovatory
approach to the English landscape has only recently
been given its full due in spite of his decades of fame.
I suspect also that his influence on Lanyon, and on
others too, was much greater than has been realised.
Since this essay was originally written I have ascer-
tained that Lanyon and Hitchens were on friendly
terms and corresponded with each other.

[10] The parallel should not be pushed too far since these
artists frequently employ an uptilted perspective,
which Nancy, as a rule, eschews in her later work.
Neither does she follow Monet in his obsession with
the interpenetration of water by light.

[11] By this I reflect no discredit on the co-ordinator of the
UCC exhibition, Hilary O'Kelly. As I remember, she
did an excellent job in terms of the limited space
available to her.

The Artist Speaks

a four-part interview with Nancy Wynne-Jones

BRIAN FALLON
with Barbara Ann Taylor

I

1922–1956: childhood in Wales; music and art studies; the war

You were born in 1922 at Dolgellau, in North Wales, into what might very loosely be called Anglo-Welsh county class. Do you feel yourself to be specifically Welsh or English, then, or not particularly either? It seems to me that there is a very definite Celtic quality in your work.

Yes, I do feel Welsh, very much so, even though my mother was English. She had been brought up in Wales, however, and I have always identified myself with my Welsh ancestors. I heard much about my Wynne-Jones forebears, and I knew that my father's family stretched back a number of generations. I was not so interested in my relatives of the previous generation who were mostly clergymen and not specially Welsh. It was a social thing, when I was young, that if you had any social pretensions you spoke English. My mother didn't allow us to learn Welsh and I regret that now, of course. I read things like the *Mabinogion*, and loved it. I was equally enthralled by Greek and Roman myths – I devoured a big book about classical mythology. Nowadays, of course, I also feel Irish.

We lived half the year in Wales, which was my mother's home, and half the year in Dorset, so that my father could hunt. My mother's father was a stockbroker, from Manchester originally, and part German. The German part of the family had been printers, from somewhere near Strasbourg, and one of them printed a book illustrated by Urs Graf. They were called Schott, but later – perhaps because of the First World War – they changed it to Scott. I'm not sure how they arrived in Manchester – it was some connection with cotton, and I think they were also in banking. They became acquainted there with a family called Taylor, who were in cotton in Bolton, and married into it. My grandmother – my mother's mother – was a Beatrice Taylor. My great-grandfather, John Leigh Taylor, had bought Penmaenucha, my home in North Wales. It was a farm really, but he added on to the house and made it a nice sort of rambling structure. It had quite a big estate – some 8,000 acres of mostly mountain land and sheep pasture. I never knew either of these grandparents because they died before I was born, but old Mr Taylor was very much loved and respected there. Even in my day, people still talked about him with affection. My grandfather moved to Penmaenucha on the death of my great-grandfather.

I believe your Schott ancestors had some connection with David Cox, the great English water-colourist.

Thornhill, Nancy Wynne-Jones' Dorset home from 1927 to 1939

NWJ's mother, Sybil Scott, aged about 11, painted by Sigismund Goetze, c.1900

NWJ's father, Charles Llewelyn Wynne-Jones, c.1914, when he was 23

Shooting party at Cregennan, Arthog, c.1910. NWJ's mother is sitting third from the left. To her left is Nancy's godmother, Topsy (Lady Gladys Williams), and grandmother, Beatrice Scott. Her grandfather, George Frederick Scott, is standing on the right, with General John Vaughan (Nancy's godfather) seated in front of him. A cousin, Jane Eardley-Wilmot, is seated on her mother's right.

NWJ's great-grandfather, John Leigh Taylor, with his daughter (Nancy's grandmother) Beatrice Scott on his left. Her grandfather, GF Scott, is seated, and the artist Sigismund Goetze reclines in the foreground. This must have been about 1900, when Goetze painted four family portraits at Penmaenucha (including top left).

Edward Scott (Great-Uncle Ted), his brother George Frederick Scott (Nancy's grandfather), their sister Great-Aunt Gretta, and their mother Sarah Ann, who had, as a girl, played the piano for Liszt

Yes, a number of them had. David Cox, I think, went on a kind of tour of the Lake District, picking up appointments as a drawing master to young ladies who had to have this accomplishment. So quite a number of county houses and families up there have David Coxes on their walls. We have one, which I think was given to my mother as her share of the Schott Coxes – there were a lot of them.

On your father's side, you are of an old Welsh family, and you even have a connection with King Edward I, haven't you?

Yes, they come from Anglesey. When Edward I killed the last prince of Wales, Llewelyn, in battle, the country more or less surrendered to him, but on the promise that he would give them a prince who spoke no English. The prince was to be shown to them publicly at Caernarvon Castle, and when it came to the day, Edward produced his baby son, who of course could speak no language of any kind. He held up the baby and said: 'Here is your prince who can speak no English.' And so he was sent to be brought up by my family in Anglesey as a kind of ward. It was the natural thing at that time to bring up aristocratic children away from their parents. It was supposed to make them tougher and build up loyalty among the aristocracy.

Anyway, after Edward returned to England, they rewarded my family with an estate on Anglesey called Treiorwerth, which means 'the house of Edward', and it – or part of it, at any rate – remained in the family over centuries. By my time it was a very nice Queen Anne house belonging to my cousins, the Wynnes, and it was still in the family until about twenty or thirty years ago.

In Wales, the gentry – for want of a better word – were divided up in earlier times into five royal and ten noble tribes, and we were one of the ten noble ones. There were no surnames in Wales until they were given them by the English in the 17th and 18th centuries. They chose Wynne as theirs, and one of the Joneses married a Wynne heiress, eventually becoming Wynne-Jones.

You also have a connection with the Vaughans, who were originally a royal family, I think.

Yes, they were a royal family. I'm not quite sure where we joined up, but we certainly intermarried at various times. And General John Vaughan, who had fought in the Boer War, was my godfather.

According to tradition, Owen Glendower, the Welsh patriot, went at one time to visit the head of the Vaughans, hoping to persuade him to join in rebellion against the English king. He and

Hywel Vaughan went out hunting together, and Glendower came back on his own. He said that they had parted company at some stage of the hunt, but the rumour sprang up that Hywel Vaughan had turned his bow and arrows against Glendower, who was wearing chainmail under his hunting costume, and that Glendower then killed Hywel Vaughan and hid his body in a hollow tree. The particular tree was even pointed out for many generations. In the 19th century it blew down, and inside it there was a human skeleton. We have a 19th-century etching of this tree.

There were various anecdotes told about General Vaughan. One concerned a copper wastepaper basket he always kept in his study, until one day a visiting archaeologist saw it and thought it looked interesting. He asked the General where he had got it, and was told that it had been dug up in the park around his house. He took it off to the Museum of Wales, where it was identified as a very rare type of Bronze Age vessel. They exhibited it there for a time, until the General rather impatiently asked for its return because he found it inconvenient to be without his wastepaper basket.

He had an old friend, an admiral, with whom he played cards once a week. He would ride over to the admiral, who lived quite close to him, on his old chestnut cob, and it didn't matter if he had a little too much to drink because the cob would see him home. One evening he had drunk rather more than usual, but still got safely home. The next morning a message came from the admiral, saying: 'Here is your storm lantern. Would you please return my parrot and cage?'

The name Vaughan reminds me of three old sisters, the Misses Vaughan – no connection of the General's – who lived in the village, and who were always in long black skirts and had geraniums in their window. I used to go down and visit them, usually with Drewie, our governess. Their cottage smelt a little, not that it was actually dirty but they never opened the windows. One day Drewie was talking of Mrs Roberts the Yard having such nice begonias. The eldest Miss Vaughan said, 'Once we had a begonia...', the second Miss Vaughan said '...in a pot...', and the third Miss Vaughan said, '...but we forgot to water it...', and the first Miss Vaughan finished, '...so it died.'

My godmother Topsy was the sister of Denys Finch-Hatton, the lover of Karen Blixen, the writer. He was a kind of daredevil who got himself killed eventually. She was a very beautiful woman, with a long grecian-style nose – exactly like the Flora in Botticelli's *Primavera* – and a lovely singing voice, very high and clear, almost like a boy soprano. She was a daughter of Lord Winchelsea, and became Gladys Williams by marriage. My other godmother was Nêst Lloyd-Williams, who had been a champion golfer in the very early days of women's golf – a round-faced woman, very weather-beaten like all golfers. A very nice pair of godmothers, I must say.

NWJ's grandfather, Dean Llewelyn Wynne-Jones, fishing at Cidwm in Snowdonia

I believe one of your Wynne-Jones ancestors fought in the Battle of Trafalgar.

That's right, my great-great-grandfather – who, incidentally, had an Irish wife – was one of Nelson's officers in the battle. He was one of the few Wynne-Joneses who weren't in the Church – that's to say, the Church of Wales. They were nearly all clergymen, including my own grandfather, my father's father, who was Dean of St Asaph. He would have been a bishop only he felt that his Welsh was not good enough. He had been a barrister before that, had studied at Trinity College Dublin, so he was a late vocation. He was a very nice man, very warm and friendly.

And then you had an aunt who was a painter.

Yes, my father's sister, my only aunt, sketched in the way that ladies of her day did. She was better than most; in a later time she would have been a good illustrator of children's books. She went down to Cornwall and studied with Stanhope Forbes for a while, and she also went to the Slade for a term or two. I don't know how she ever got her parents to allow her to do that. Girls of her generation, you know, were not expected to do anything.

    She was unmarried, and somehow the quintessential auntie figure – smallish and round-faced, white-haired, and very gentle. I loved her. She used to make up stories for me about her brass elephant, Ellie, and my bronze mouse, Whiskers. They used to go on adventures together. Auntie Dolly used to make up little books of these stamp books one had then. She'd put paper inside them and write a story on it, and it would be illustrated, and there would be a covering on the stamp book. She gave them to me and I so loved them. I kept them for years. I wish I had them still.

Did your own home have any art on the walls?

It didn't have any contemporary art. Or anything contemporary at all really. We had photographs of it as it was in the days when my grandmother was a young woman, and it was exactly the same; even the furniture was in the same places. It was good 18th-century and Regency furniture, and on the walls were a lot of so-called Old Masters bought by my Great-Uncle Charles, the rich man of the family. He bought all these – as he thought – Cuyps and van de Veldes. None of them was what they were claimed to be, though they were reasonable enough paintings of that period, but dullish.

Sybil Wynne-Jones with
Alec, Ronnie (Polly) and
Esperance (Nancy), c.1924

Great-Uncle Charlie had no children of his own, so my father, who was a parson's son, had become his heir. He was sent to Eton and then was put into a very expensive cavalry regiment. He married my mother, who was a fairly wealthy heiress, while still in the army, but left it when his father-in-law died so that he could manage the estate. Great-Uncle Charlie died soon after that, and it was found that he had spent all he had. In spite of the fact that it was a love match which lasted all their lives, my father always felt guilty of having married a rich woman under false pretences.

Had your parents any particular interest in art?

No, not really. They were interested in furniture, and my mother always had a yearning for a flower painting, which eventually my father gave her – a very poor one, I thought, but she was very pleased with it. They didn't go to concerts or exhibitions, or know the names of anybody contemporary at all. But my mother was a great reader, with a very good library. I was actually christened Esperance, because my mother had read a book called *Miss Esperance and Mr Wycherley* and had fallen in love with the name. She was particularly interested in history and poetry. She even wrote poetry herself, which was quite good in a traditional way. When – I think it must have been after one of the children was born – she had a kind of nervous breakdown, our doctor in Wales, Dr JR Heath, read some of her poetry and encouraged her to write more and get it published, which she did. She had her own little sitting-room where she used to go and write.

She was interested in photography as well. I think she must have learned it from my grandmother. That was another thing Dr Heath helped her with, because he himself was a very keen amateur photographer. Dr Heath was a wonderful man, a fine musician, but interested in all the arts. I owe him a lot myself.

There was a strange episode when I was four or five years old and I became quite ill – perhaps originally with flu. My mother grew worried about me because I was ill for so long and wasn't getting better, or didn't seem to have much interest in anything. So she hired this harper to play outside my bedroom – I suppose to cheer or distract me. He came from Barmouth and was the last of the old itinerant harpers of Wales. He sat under a tree on the lawn, just outside my window, an old white-haired man in a long coat, and I could see him as well as hear him. He had a big harp, not a small one, and it seemed to me that he played for quite a long time. It was traditional Welsh music. I recognised some of the tunes, including *David of the White Rock*. At any rate, I seemed to get better after that

You were educated at home, I think.

Yes, because I was considered rather delicate. I was educated by a governess called Miss Drew, who had, I think, originally been brought into the family to prepare my brothers for prep school. She wasn't that much older than myself – say fifteen or sixteen years – so she was a friend. Drewie, as we all called her, was interested in the arts. She wasn't an intellectual person, or profound in any way, but she had a great love of music. And she had been brought up next door to the Skeaping family in Kent – Jack Skeaping, the sculptor, and Ken, who was a cellist with one of the big orchestras, and their sister Joan who was a ballerina. They were a slightly bohemian family and had one wall which all the children were allowed to draw on when they were small. And so this, for me, was a contact with... I suppose you'd call it an arty kind of life.

Drewie took me to tea once with Jack Skeaping. I must have been nine or ten, I suppose, and I was very excited to meet a real artist, a man who painted horses, because that's what I liked to do. And he gave me quite a big drawing of a pony, which unfortunately has been lost over the years.

Basically, I led a rather socially narrow life, with lessons in the morning and so on. I used to walk around the woods and fields, just looking at things, particularly the animals and birds. I was very upset by the fact that the wild creatures were so frightened of man, and I would sit on a gate hoping that the birds and other things would come closer me. Sometimes they did, in fact. I would get up at four or five on a summer morning and sit by a tree, watching the foxcubs come out to play. I was the only member of my family who did this. Nature was my companion. Perhaps this is what made me a painter.

Victoria Drew (Drewie), NWJ's governess and life-long friend, c.1935

JR Heath, c.1930

ESPERANCE.

Nancy Wynne-Jones, c.1933

Juvenilia
1934/35, watercolour on paper,
35.5 × 53 cm (14 × 21 in)

So you moved between Wales and Dorset every year. That must have been quite an operation, especially in those days.

We had a kind of Tolstoyan removal every year. First of all, ahead of us would go the butler and the head housemaid, and probably one of the other housemaids, to prepare the house for us. They would take quite a lot with them, things like the cutlery and silver. They all went off by train. And about a fortnight later, the family would move in procession – first of all the car with my parents and some of the children in it, and secondly a big sort of station wagon driven by the chauffeur, with another child and masses and masses of boxes and the dogs in baskets and the canary in its cage. And we all trooped off.

You drew and painted from very early in life, I think. Who were your first teachers?

I was always very interested in painting and drawing, so my mother organised classes for me in Sherborne in Dorset. Ruth Gervis, an illustrator of children's books, gave these classes once a week, which lasted for the whole of the afternoon. I was about nine when I started. She used to bring into her classroom real animals to paint – a guinea-pig, a rabbit, and other things. At other times we would do flowers, or we would go outside and paint. I remember going to Sherborne Castle to paint it, for example. She was an excellent teacher, with real enthusiasm, and she insisted on close observation, that you really looked at what you saw. She made me aware of the necessity of truth to nature. That lesson has lasted me all my life.

Mrs Gervis belonged to the Royal Drawing Society, so every term she would send up several drawings from each of us to the Society's head office. In turn, they would make comments and send these in, which was of interest, of course. And then once a year there was a big national exhibition, and we were encouraged by Mrs Gervis to get together a sort of portfolio of our best paintings. These went up for possible prizes and medals, and I won a number of bronze medals.

But you were not trained then in oil paints, surely?

No, in watercolour. Ruth Gervis gave us drawing boards and paper. She also trained me to take art in the Schools Certificate exam, and to draw still life. She insisted, too, that we draw cleanly and not smudge things, and we were trained to hatch in the old way, which was good for us. Even at that age, I thought that one day I would be a professional artist.

You have said several times that the opening-up of your mind, intellectually and artistically, was largely the work of Dr Heath in Wales.

That was when I was several years older – I must have been about thirteen then. JR Heath was a great friend of my parents and he used to come to dinner in our house quite often. He and my father were keen fisherman and talked about fishing. My mother showed him poetry I had written and pictures I had painted – imaginary landscapes, which he thought were interesting. I was rather isolated for anyone to talk to about these things, and so he used to take me on his rounds sometimes. He visited patients on remote farms at the tops of mountains, and he'd take me along in the car and talk to me about music or painting or poetry. He knew everything that was happening in the arts.

Dr Heath had bad asthma, which was the main reason he lived in the countryside. Otherwise I think he would have had a lot more to do with the musical world. He composed and played the violin, among other things. He used to come back in the evenings, at the end of his rounds, and play halfway through the night, which meant also that he drank quite a lot to keep awake. At any rate, he died when he was not much past sixty.

Did he influence you to become a music student?

It was largely through his influence that I became tremendously interested in music in the first place. I was about fifteen when I became enamoured of the violin. I used to go into Bournemouth, about thirty miles away, for lessons with the first violinist of the Bournemouth Symphony Orchestra, Harold Fairhurst. He was a good teacher, but of course I was too old really to become good at it. You should start learning the violin at about six years old; after that, your hands tend to stiffen up.

I also began to compose music, again encouraged by Dr Heath, who had conducted his own compositions several time in the Prom concerts. He also conducted the Halle Orchestra occasionally, and at one stage he'd been one of the white hopes of British music. Dr Heath taught me harmony and the other basic things. He was the greatest help to me in so many ways, because my brothers were away at school and my parents were not really interested in all that, so he was the only person I could talk to about the arts.

So you were still at home with your parents and your governess at this time, and your brothers were at school.

My brothers were away at boarding school. Of course, we would all go up to Wales from Dorset just in time for the summer holidays. And we used to stay in a wooden bungalow built by my grandparents up in the mountains at Cregennan, on two small lakes, for trout-fishing. We used to go up

there without any servants and look after ourselves – cooked for by Drewie, who thoroughly enjoyed it. To be there without any of the staff was exciting for us in itself.

In the summers my brothers' friends, and my father's friends with their wives, would come to Penmaenucha for shooting. There was a continual coming and going. And, of course, we had friends in the neighbourhood whom we played tennis with and so on, or pottered about with in boats.

And as a child in Dorset, did you hunt?

I hunted until I was about twelve, but I never really liked it. My father and my brothers were all keen horsemen and huntsmen, but although I quite liked riding, I could get bored, and out hunting I was frightened by all those great big jumps. And so, when I was old enough to admit that, I gave it up.

During term time I did extra classes in Sherborne, because by that time I had rather outgrown Drewie intellectually. So I went to these extra classes, to prepare myself for the Schools Certificate. The classes were given by private teachers. I went to a lady called Miss Stay, who had been a governess herself in her day. I used to spend the day there and have lessons with her in the morning, with a couple of other girls. And I would have lunch with them and then probably go on to a drawing class, or perhaps piano lessons, in the afternoon.

The Second World War must have bulked hugely in your life, especially since you lost your two brothers in it. You also saw some war service yourself, on the Home Front.

I was sixteen when war broke out. My father, who had been a cavalry officer, was recalled to the War Office in London, and my eldest brother was already in the army. My younger brother was at

Penmaenucha from the air: NWJ was born in the bedroom whose window tops the large gable

NWJ and her mother on the garden steps at Penmaenucha, 1926

NWJ on her pony, Brownie, at Thornhill, Dorset, c.1935

Oxford, and he was to join up at Easter. So my mother and I stayed on in Wales for the time being, and I took violin lessons in Aberystwyth. I used to go there on a little train journey every week.

I was a VAD – a 'voluntary auxiliary detachment' – as well as a nurse. I did the nursing course with a friend of mine, Elizabeth Russell, one of a family which lived near us. She was about my age, and we used to go into the local hospital for our practical training. We were present at operations, which I must say horrified me because I found that people groaned under anaesthetics. They swore they couldn't feel anything, but still they were moaning, which was very frightening.

By then I had more or less decided that music was to be my career, so I went to London and attended the Royal Academy of Music, to study the violin and composition. You had to take two instruments and one of them had to be the piano, so I took the violin for my first one and the piano as my second. For violin I was with Marjorie Heywood, who had a quartet of her own, and for composition with Norman Demuth. Demuth was a modern composer, reasonably well known then, who wrote a lot of ballets and that sort of thing, and he encouraged me to be atonal, which was quite daring at the time. He had great hopes of me, and though technically I was pretty sketchy, he said: 'Well, if you can run before you can walk, why don't you run for a while?' I had a few things performed by the college orchestra. I also wrote one piece for piano and clarinet – an odd combination, when I think of it. The other pieces were orchestral.

I wasn't considered promising as a violinist, but I had acquired a certain competence and was able to play in chamber groups and in the school orchestra. We had fortnightly concerts, but in between we naturally had practice and rehearsals, and very often we would rehearse under student conductors as well. And the boys at the back of the orchestra – we would have a long series of umpah-umpah passages, and they would be playing *Pop Goes the Weasel* and all kinds of things, because you couldn't hear yourself.

Who were your fellow students?

Nobody who became very famous. There was Bryan Balkwill, who was a friend of mine. He played piano in my piece for clarinet and piano. He was composing himself at the time, and afterwards he became quite a well-known conductor, at Covent Garden and at the Wexford Festival. And there was a very good cellist called Peter Halley, who I think went out to Australia eventually. He was a marvellous player. When Mr Demuth went off to the war, I went to William Alwyn, a well-known composer of film and incidental music. A very nice man, I got on very well with him.

Meanwhile I was in London in the Blitz, with bombs zooming down. When I was nineteen, I knew I would be called up soon, so a cousin of mine, Katherine Scott, came up with a plan. She and her brother Phil had a flat in London – they were my idea of a bohemian, art-loving household. When it came near the time for me to be called up, Katherine suggested to my parents that I would be unhappy in any of the armed forces, so why didn't I volunteer as a draughtswoman for the Ordnance Survey? It had been sent up from Southampton to Esher, to avoid the danger of being along the coast. So I did that, and they accepted me. My parents and I were living in a hotel near Ham Common then.

How long were you doing that? And was it very demanding?

For the rest of the war – about five years. You were given blueprints and you had to put in blue for a river and red for a road. I often had visions of soldiers marching up to a river and holding rifles up to their heads, because I had filled in what should have been a river in red! These were maps of France, and some of them may have been used in the Normandy Landings. After a while I was sec-

onded to the section where they were making diagrams for charts of the maps. I enjoyed this work much more, because you could colour them more or less as you liked. I also had access to pencils and paint and all sorts of things, and I used to draw little pictures of my own on the white card we were given. We certainly were not overworked!

And all this was during the Blitz?

Yes, it was. We were in a block of flats in Chesham Place, before we moved to Ham Common, and I remember the first time the bombers came over to bomb the City of London. Everybody rushed to the roof of the building to see the fires. That didn't last for long, as they gradually started bombing all the rest of London as well. In the daytime, if you were in a shop when the alarm went off, they would lock you in until the all-clear, and that might be hours. And at night the bombers came over regularly, at about nine o'clock, and the people who owned the block of flats had arranged mattresses on shelves of the luggage room so we could all sleep down in the basement.

Because I was so young, I had a top bunk right under the ceiling, which was a great big concrete slab. And when I heard the bombs coming down – you could hear them, you know, whistling down – I would look up at this and think, 'I don't fancy that very much!' But after the Blitz was over – well, because of it really – we moved out to stay with cousins at Gerrard's Cross, and I was able to link up with the trains for my classes.

And were you playing the violin and composing all through this?

No, I had given up the violin because it was impossible to practice. But I remember that I wrote a piece of music which was in memoriam for my brothers – for the family really. My teacher thought it was very good, though I never actually had it played because it was too difficult for a student orchestra. But I gradually dried up doing any of these things because of the death of my brothers, which was such a tremendous shock.

Both were killed in the war – one in action and the other accidentally. My oldest brother, Alec, was killed in Cyrenaica, in north Africa. He was an officer in the 60th Rifles, and he was sent out to capture a machine-gun position. A German officer came out with a white flag, Alec stood up to take the surrender, and the German officer shot him. The men with him were taken prisoner. Alec was listed as missing for ages; nobody knew what had happened to him.

Ronnie – we called him Polly – was serving in the Royal Dragoons as a cavalry officer. He and his men had just captured a machine-gun when it went off and shot him through the heart. The two deaths came within a year of each other.

Did you find that your responsibility to your parents weighed heavily on you, since you were now their only child?

To a certain extent it did, yes. I did feel I had to look after them and that I had to take care of myself. I remember once I was very ill with measles, which can be a dangerous thing if you're an adult. I had a temperature of 106 degrees, and I remember lying on the bed feeling as if I could just drop off into unconsciousness, and thinking, 'No, I mustn't do that, because if I do I might die, and I can't put that on my parents. I have to stay awake and fight it.'

My parents had sold up in Dorset by this time, so there was no house there. They were living in Wales, but they understood that I would stay on in London. I had always said that I wanted to when I grew up, and they accepted it. I shared a flat with Drewie for some time. She had been in the Auxiliary Territorial Service, the ATS, during the war – she was a major – and when she came out she got a job as housekeeper to the Fishmongers' Company, in charge of banquets and everything. She had a lovely flat which she didn't live in, but after a time we both wanted a flat on our own, so she went back to hers in the Fishmongers' place, and I to mine in Chelsea.

At this stage I could neither paint nor compose. My creative energies were dried up. Since I knew about books, I got this little bookshop on the Fulham Road – the Forum Bookshop – which I

Ronald (Polly) Wynne-Jones, 1940

Charles Alexander (Alec) Wynne-Jones, 1938

ran with the help of an old friend from Wales. My father paid for it, although I had a fairly big allowance. It had been owned by the son of AA Milne – at least I always thought so, because his name was CR Milne and I had heard that Christopher Robin had a bookshop. I never asked him about it, though, because I had heard that he very much disliked being remembered as Christopher Robin. He was a shy, quiet man.

And how did that venture go, the bookshop?

It was never very successful as a bookshop, mainly because I bought the books I liked myself, but it was interesting because of the people I met through it. Osbert Sitwell was a fairly regular customer – quite a pleasant man, very courteous and dignified. Steward Grainger, the film actor, used to come in as well. So did Peter Cushing – both of them extremely nice and unaffected. We had a little lending library, and there was an old admiral who would take a book out and then bring it back quickly because there wasn't enough sex in it. He would say, 'No good, no good. Boy's book.'

My lease ran out and I rented another shop near Harrod's, in Beauchamp Place – a very smart place now. And that was hopeless because I could never compete with the Harrod's stock, but by then I had begun to paint much more, and quite seriously.

Who or what first really oriented you towards Modernism in art, or contemporary art, shall we say? Was there any individual milestone, or some particular illumination?

Shortly before the war, when I was about fifteen, I had come across Herbert Read's book *Art Now*. I was totally fascinated by it, and I remained so for years. Largely through reading that I began as an abstract painter. It didn't occur to me that abstract painters had arrived at their images only through years of work and thought. Still, it was exciting for a young artist, thinking that you were doing something entirely new. It was very formal abstraction, quite geometric. Mondrian was one of my models.

Art Now had little essays in it on a number of contemporary artists, mostly either abstract or surrealist. Barbara Hepworth must have been in it, and of course Ben Nicholson. And for some reason, I remember a French painter named Hélion, a very second-generation kind of abstract painter really. I was immensely excited by this book; it seemed to open up a whole new world for me. The fact that you could think of art as a subject in itself, that you didn't have to produce a likeness of something, that shapes and colours were exciting in themselves – all that came as a revelation to me.

And all that occurred to you at fifteen or so? That's remarkable.

Yes, but it didn't occur to me that these painters had not arrived at what I admired so much without having studied the natural world very closely and deciding what they wanted to use from it. I believed they had found these shapes for themselves to begin with, had arrived at their statement more or less straight off. And I thought, 'well, this is how you paint', and that it was imagined out of your head, just like that.

But moving ahead again... While I was sharing the flat with Drewie, a ground-floor one in Pimlico, there was a woman called Barbara Shaw living in one of the other flats. She was an illustrator – quite a good illustrator – and she and I became friendly. She saw one or two of the small landscapes, based on the square, which I was painting then, and she suggested that I might like to go to Heatherley's Art School. So in the end I gave up the bookshop and I went to Heatherley's, which was a well-known, open art school, and long established. It's still going strong. It didn't have a formal course; it was more like an atelier. There were classes and models, you came and went, and they instructed you in a certain way. They would have life models one day, still life the next, and imaginative painting or something the next day again, and you could choose your own subject. You weren't aiming at a diploma or anything.

There were some surprising people there from time to time. Jim Dine, for instance, used to come and draw, though I never knew him. The others were mostly rather elderly, what you'd call Sunday painters.

NWJ in the Forum
Bookshop, Fulham Road,
with Bryn, c.1950

I was there for about a year. And to my surprise, I found that I was awfully good at it and was much acclaimed by the tutors. If there was one on duty, he would bring all the others along to have a look at my work. So I was extremely surprised by it all, but of course encouraged and excited too.

Was that the first time you had painted in oils?

Yes, it was in fact. They were life paintings and drawings – the very first time I had attempted such a thing. I was living in a small house in Chelsea when I met a painter called Derek Middleton, with whom I had a tenuous kind of affair. He lived on a barge just by one of the Thames bridges, which I thought very glamorous. He suggested that I should go to Chelsea Art School, so I left Heatherley's after a year and went there instead. Not immediately, though – there was a little gap between the two when I worked on my own. The people in Chelsea asked me if I wanted to take a diploma course, and I said no. I really worked in much the same way as before, just for myself, with some tuition. I was there for three years – 1954 or 1955 was my last year.

Did Middleton have a circle of painter-friends whom you could mix with?

He did, yes. He had been in the war and was very friendly with a man called Peter Kinley, whom I got to know well. They had both been in Intelligence. Derek had a joint exhibition in a Brooke Street gallery with Kinley, Albert Irvin and Anthony Whishaw. His own painting was heavily influenced by Kinley, who was very much into de Stael about that time. You know the kind of thing – all done with a palette-knife, squares of very heavily matiered paint. He did it well enough, though there wasn't anything particularly original about it.

Bert Irvin was doing large, rather expressionistic pictures of animals, and sometimes he did one of his little daughter in a chair – all heavily painted. He lived in one room in his mother-in-law's house in Putney with his wife and baby, and probably found it pretty difficult, so he was out as much as he could. We became very friendly, and remain so after all these years.

Who were your teachers in Chelsea?

One teacher was Prunella Clough, whom I found very interesting. She was a shy woman – rather intellectual, but interesting. I was only in her class once or twice. I suppose my big influence there was a man called Edward Wakeford, a part-Polish writer and painter – actually, a very good painter in a figurative way. I'm sure he'll be rediscovered one of these days. He was a sort of realist, about as realist as Lowry, say, but very different, much more cultured and human. He was very self-effacing, but if you knew him at all well you found he was highly intelligent and amusing, a very fine man with an original mind. He took a great interest in my work, which he thought very promising. He encouraged me to be free with my brushstrokes and to use colour.

Edward was born on the Isle of Man – his father was a vicar there – and later, when I was living in Cornwall, he wrote a book about his early years on the Isle of Man, which was absolutely brilliant. There was also a Polish woman at Chelsea named Olga Karchevskaya, whom I became friendly with. She was married to Marcelli Karchevsky, who had been editor of the Polish equivalent to the London *Times*, which he ran for the exiled Poles in London. He was a lovely man, tremendous, very much the Continental intellectual, and had a great sense of humour.

Olga was great fun, and she and I and Edward used to talk together a lot. Edward was deaf, and he used to cross the room to us commenting on someone's work. He'd say in a loud voice: 'She's no idea of what she's doing, you know, no idea of what she's trying to do!'

Did he show in any of the leading London galleries? Was he in the Royal Academy, for instance?

I think he showed in the Academy, yes. He certainly had a West End show after I left Chelsea, I think in Cork Street, or near it. He didn't exhibit very often, you know, he was a perfectionist worker. Edward must have died just at the end of the sixties, or the early seventies. He was a very delicate man physically. He used to come sometimes to my parties, but he had a bad heart and wasn't really able for much of this kind of thing.

Was it about this time that you started to travel abroad, or was it before that?

I think it was about then. I had read a book about Portugal called *The Blue Moon*, or something like that, and I thought I'd like to go there. I talked to Barbara Shaw about it. She had also read the book and wanted to go to Portugal too. So we decided to go together, and that was certainly while I was at Chelsea, because I remember showing Edward all the little watercolours – I did watercolour stick and oil in Chelsea – and some oils I had done from my visit. He was enthusiastic about them, and I recognise now, with hindsight, that the Portuguese trip was important for my later development. Unfortunately, I lost an awful lot of works from that time because I sent them to be framed by Greene's in Chelsea, which was a famous art shop. They had a big fire there, and my Portuguese paintings – or most of them anyway – disappeared in the flames.

When did you become interested in Italian painting? I know it has meant a great deal to you over the years.

I was staying with my parents one time, and I was reading a book about Tintoretto. I was reading a lot about the Renaissance artists then, about all artists before me really. This book had reproductions of a lot of the things in San Rocco in Venice. I thought I'd love to see them, and then it dawned on me that there was no reason why I shouldn't. Once again I rang up Barbara, one of the few people I knew who was usually able or willing to drop everything and just come abroad. So we went off to Italy and we stayed in Venice, and from there we travelled to Padua and Mantua and various other places. This was not solely in pursuit of Tintoretto; there was so much to see besides him, and so much that was good and exciting.

Edward Wakeford in the 1950s

Albert Irvin, Zennor, 1958

The Tintorettos in San Rocco I found quite overwhelming, but I also discovered Carpaccio for myself. I was walking around some of those alleyways that are everywhere in Venice, and suddenly there was this church which turned out to contain quite a number of his paintings. One of them was a St George, and another was of St Jerome in his study – though now they say it's really St Augustine. The church itself was called San Giorgio dei' Schiavoni, and was founded originally by Dalmatians. Carpaccio was really the first one to paint that particular golden Venetian light. I know that the Flemish artists had a big influence on early Venetian painting, but the light and space in Carpaccio is entirely different from theirs. His is a more intuitive grasp of space, you might say, whereas theirs is more calculated. For a north European, the discovery of true southern light is a revelation. You realise that it is a substance in its own right, a whole dimension to things. In our own cloudy climates you are simply not aware of it most of the time.

I didn't much like the big Titian *Assumption in the Frari*; that side of Titian doesn't interest me at all. I prefer some of the big portraits. Mantegna I found very powerful, and I still admire him a lot. Bellini I didn't see much of, as I remember. Some of the earlier Tintorettos, the ones in the Palazzo Ducale for instance, also impressed me, but his very late work, above all, is immensely visionary and powerful.

We made an expedition out to Torcello, an island in the lagoon, to see the famous Byzantine-style Madonna there. What impressed me about Torcello itself was that it was so rural. You went up to the old church where the Madonna was, and on the way there were goats grazing around you, great patches of artichokes growing, and all sorts of wild flowers. And – a typical Italian touch – in the middle of a vegetable patch there would be a single iris or rose standing up. Then you walked into the small crumbling church and this tremendous mosaic rose directly above your head.

One of the things which struck me most about Venice was that instead of being a romantic, dreamy sort of place, it was very much a port, with the smell of the sea everywhere, and quite noisy too. The Venetians themselves seemed to be rather a noisy, extrovert people who talked or shouted to each other a lot – a bit like the Cornish!

How and why did you finish with Chelsea? Did you feel it could help you no further?

I had begun to work much more on my own, and as I remember, Edward ceased teaching there about that time, I think probably for health reasons. There didn't seem much point in staying on. I thought I would rather work at home. I had bought a lovely little house in Chelsea, in Bywater Street. It was the end house in the street, so it had windows facing in all directions. I had a little studio there, where I worked away on my own.

I was painting some landscapes in oils but they were very abstract, except for the odd self-portrait or something like that. All the painting I was really interested in was very abstract, very linear – quite thin, you might say. So I hadn't really managed to put down what my eye saw with any kind of personal feeling. I just wasn't able to deal with the landscape directly; it was altogether too overwhelming. In my painting it came out awfully academic, and I wasn't interested in that. I wasn't able to build up sufficient confidence to have some kind of dialogue between myself and the subject.

Was that perhaps a hangover from the war years?

I think probably it was, yes – an unwillingness to try anything which could come too close to me. I didn't have a positive energy, so to speak.

The affair with Derek Middleton seems to have lasted over two years.

It must have, looking back, but it ended rather spectacularly by dragging in two friends I had known from childhood in Wales – Elizabeth and Johnny Russell, who lived just around the corner from me in Chelsea. Elizabeth worked in the bookshop with me, and Johnny had been in the war and known Derek – he'd also been in Intelligence. He was married to a girl called Verity. Derek and I, and Johnny and Verity, used to meet every Sunday in the Six Bells, and then we'd spend the rest of the day together. And unfortunately Derek and Verity fell violently in love, and Verity went off with Derek. I was terribly upset and Johnny was terribly upset, and Elizabeth was dreadfully upset – there were reverberations in all directions. That happened about 1956, I think.

Did you carry on painting, in the meantime, more or less as before?

Yes, I carried on painting, but without any kind of breakthrough. I don't think I was aware I hadn't achieved that though; I imagined that what I was doing was quite good and avant garde. Bert Irvin and the others seemed to think so too.

With Nicholson and Hepworth down in Cornwall most of the time, I take it that the dominant, or at least fashionable, figures in the London art world would have been Graham Sutherland, Keith Vaughan, Ivon Hitchens, Matthew Smith, and a few others. Augustus John had largely faded out by then, and Francis Bacon was still a relative outsider.

Yes, I was slightly interested in Sutherland, whose pictures of roots and other organic things seemed to me to be part of English nature mysticism – the kind of thing you find in Richard Jefferies and certain people like that. Alan Reynolds was another painter working in that area, but I never cared for him. And Matthew Smith disappointed me. I had expected to like his paintings, but when I saw them I felt that the colour was much too hot. Hitchens I didn't fully appreciate until much later.

I became quite interested at first in the Kitchen Sink School – Bratby and Middleditch and so on – though their pictures were rather one-dimensional in the end. But for me so much of the excitement of that whole London milieu was concentrated in the gallery run by Helen Lessore – the Beaux Arts, I think it was called. It had an almost primitive atmosphere and it looked like an attic, always very dark, while most of the other London galleries were like brightly lit showrooms. Helen Lessore was courageous as well in the choice of people she showed, even a little eccentric at times. Francis Bacon showed there well before he became famous. She mounted a Patrick Hayman show, in about 1959, which I went to see. It was a really good exhibition, though it wasn't a great success with the public. Somehow, Hayman never really caught on in England, whereas in Canada he did very well.

At the end of your time in London, who else was in your circle of friends?

Well, I knew the sculptor Elizabeth Frink. Derek had met her in Finches pub, and also in the Queen's Elm, where I used to go. He introduced her to me there. She was a magnificent-looking woman, with a head like a Roman emperor, and extremely nice and rather shy. She used to come to my parties with her then husband, Michel Jammet, who used to sit glowering in a corner while Liz danced. She asked me to her wedding reception in the Cavalry Club, of which my father was a member – a very staid kind of place. All the habitués of the Chelsea pubs streamed in, to the horror of the old colonels! I also knew Norbert Lynton, the critic, and his wife – both of them young and unknown at the time. She was a sculptor then. And of course, Jeff Knuttel, who was a friend of Bert Irvin's.

———

Early Paintings

Juvenilia
1935/36, watercolour on paper, 53 × 35.5 cm (21 × 14 in)

THE ROYAL DRAWING SOCIETY
EXHIBITION OF DRAWINGS, 1937.
Sherborne
Mrs Theophil Gwin's Class
Esperance Wynn-Jones.
Animals 7-35   AGE
                    13-14

Bronze Star, R.D.S.

Ordnance Survey Abstract
c.1940, watercolour on paper, 25.5 × 21.5 cm (10 × 8.5 in)

Diffws
1952, oil on canvas, 25.5 x 35.5 cm (10 x 14 in)

Self-Portrait
1953, oil on board, 46 × 30.5 cm (18 × 12 in)

Mountains and Olive Trees (Portugal)
1956, watercolour on paper, 20 × 25.5 cm (8 × 10 in)

Monastery (Portugal)
1956, watercolour on paper, 20 x 25.5 cm (8 x 10 in)

Peter Lanyon
1957, oil on board, 61 × 56 cm (24 × 22 in)

Roger Hilton
1957, oil on canvas, 76 × 63.5 cm (30 × 25 in)

Levant Mine
1958, egg tempera on paper, 38 x 25.5 cm (15 x 10 in)

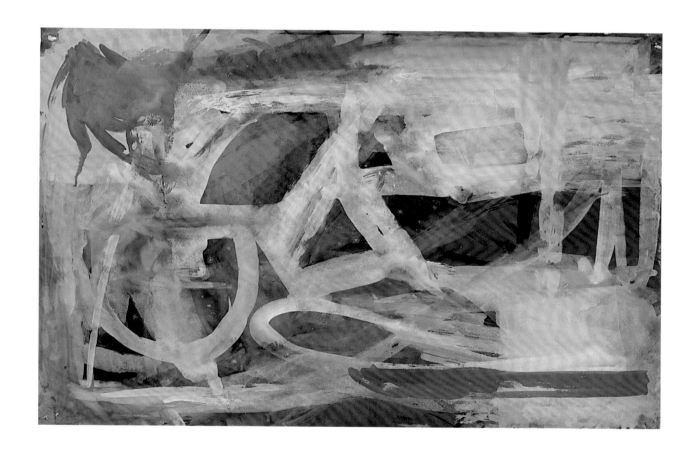

Blue Coast
1958, egg tempera on paper, 25.5 × 38 cm (10 × 15 in)

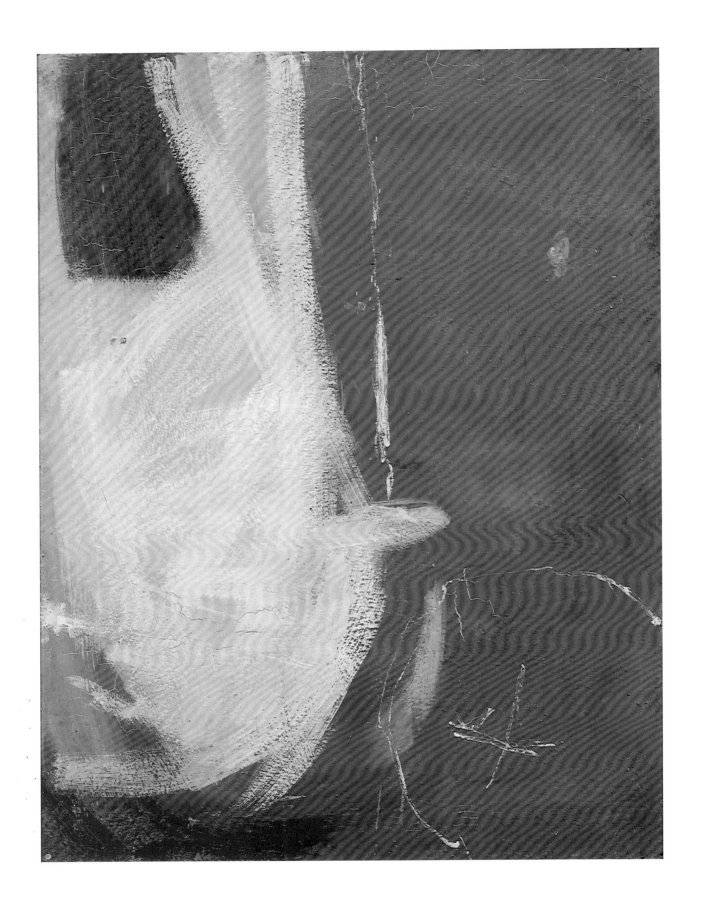

Ochre Painting
1960, oil on board, 122 x 91.5 cm (48 x 36 in)

Levant
1959, oil on board, 91.5 x 122 cm (36 x 48 in)

Nude
1960, oil on board, 152 × 122 cm (60 × 48 in)

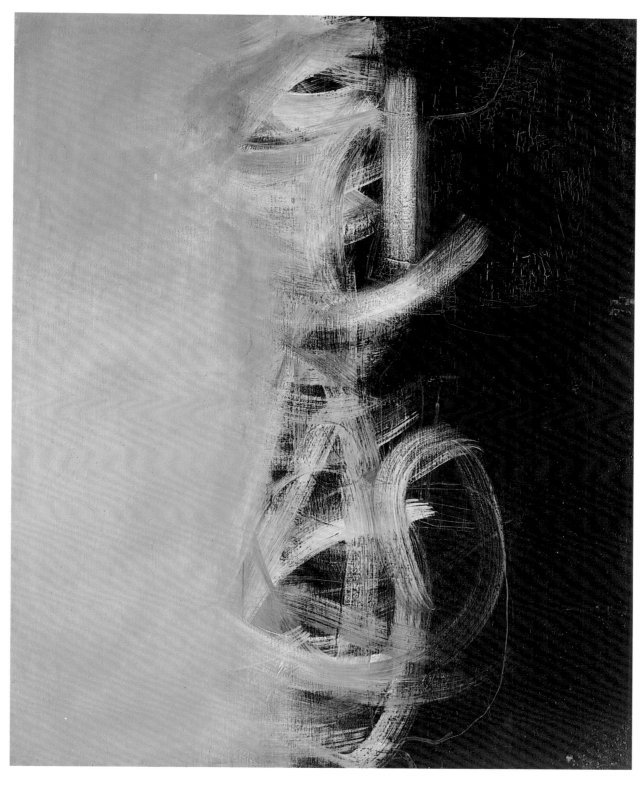

Edge
1963, oil on canvas, 127 x 102 cm (50 x 40 in)

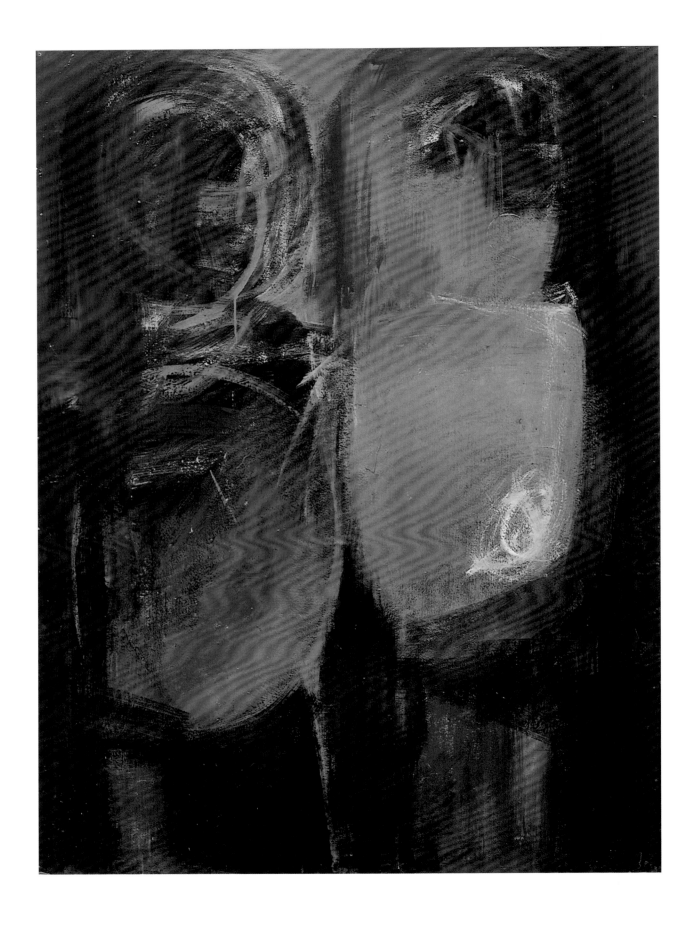

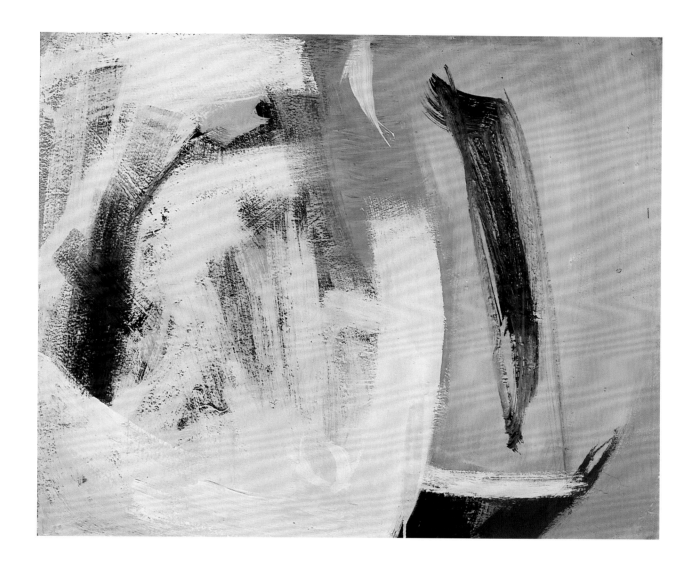

Tuareg
1961, oil on board, 168 × 122 cm (66 × 48 in)

Going Up (Sea and Land)
1960, oil on board, 51 × 63.5 cm (20 × 25 in)

II

1957–1962: the discovery of Cornwall; study under Lanyon

Tell me how you first went to Cornwall, a highlight in your career.

Before we broke up, Derek Middleton had suggested that I might be interested in going down there sometime to study with Peter Lanyon. He was interested in Lanyon's work, though it didn't seem to have made any impression on his own painting, and I myself thought it was interesting and that maybe I could learn something.

I had read a little about Lanyon in art magazines and I saw the odd picture of his at Gimpel's in London. I knew too that he ran a kind of informal school in St Ives called St Peter's Loft. It used to advertise in *Art News*, and I saw an ad saying that Lanyon was one of the teachers there, so I wrote and booked myself in for two weeks. Instead, I stayed for fifteen years.

A major turning-point in your life, of course.

Absolutely. By then I had decided that landscape was what I would like to do, though it would be a very abstract kind of landscape. And, of course, landscape with a fairly free treatment was an essential part of the St Ives style.

And how or when did you meet Peter Lanyon for the first time?

I came up the slope to where the school was, and at the top was Bill Redgrave talking to this big, blonde, handsome young man. I was just about to walk past when the man smiled and stopped me and said 'good morning', or something like that. I said – rather formally, because I'd come from London – 'Are you Mr Lanyon?'. And he said he was, and asked me a little about what I'd been doing. I had a little abstract painting with me which he was mildly interested in; he obviously saw something there. And that was how I began. Of course, everybody called him Peter.

It was a kind of revelation to me, you know, the whole St Ives 'thing', the informality and the way all the painters knew each other, and they were nearly all youngish at that time, in their thirties. The whole thing somehow was so informal, and so special.

St Ives from the air: the Island is the end of the peninsula, beyond the harbour and town. NWJ lived at the Battery, the highest point of the Island (photos: Skyviews Aerial Archives)

Peter Lanyon – typically grinding colours
(photo: Andrew Lanyon)

opposite

Peter Lanyon (in black beret) teaching at St Peter's Loft, c.1957
(photo: *The Sketch*, London)

How does Lanyon's work look to you today? And how, for that matter, does the whole St Ives School seem now, in your eyes?

Lanyon still looks tremendously original and exciting to me, though St Ives painting as a whole seems to have receded greatly. At that time, I felt, all of us there felt that we were daring and futuristic, that we were pushing the boundaries of modern art, but now most of these people seem part of the time. Even Lanyon's arrangement of the landscape looks to me, at times, quite arbitrary. I'm fully aware that in his best work a kind of whole new dimension is brought in, but for me a landscape must still look to some extent like the place which excited you in the first place.

Did you live in the little fishing town itself?

At first I lodged with Boots Redgrave. Her real name was Mary, but everybody called her Boots. She was a friendly woman who knew everybody. By the way, she has just died, so I heard. They had arranged things in the Loft so that the staff included both traditional artists like Bill Redgrave, her husband, and avant-garde ones like Lanyon. She lived on Island Road in Downalong, the old part of St Ives. Many of the roads there broke into steps going down to the harbour, and there were charming little squares of old houses. It was the local fisherman's part of town and there were a number of tall, simple buildings there with large spaces for drying the big nets. A lot of the buildings were taken over by artists when the fishing industry died, and Downalong became the place where we all lived. Only Peter, who was born in St Ives, lived elsewhere in a particularly nice house on the other side of the town.

Boots and Bill had knocked two houses on Island Road together into one, with the kitchen in the middle. The house was arranged so that Boots had her own sitting-room for herself and the children, while the students had their own on the other side. It was a kind of meeting place for artists and all sorts of people who would drop in. Boots ran a small restaurant there for a time, which she called Dauber's, after her dog. People very often came in from the pubs to chat, so it was a marvellously lively place to be.

Tell me about St Peter's Loft.

It had been an old sail loft, which is now the Penwith, or part of it is, and part of it later became a studio for Peter Rainsford. It was big and airy and spacious, and each student had a little section to himself or herself, with an easel and a table and chair. Still lifes were set up and you could draw and paint them or not, as you chose. About once a week there was a life model, but otherwise you just did what you wanted to. You could even work outside, then come back and finish it in the studio. One or other of the painter-teachers would come in every day and look at your work and correct it, or help you if necessary.

There were almost never more than half a dozen people there. Some of them were people sent by the British Council to study in St Ives for maybe a month. A lot of the students came from Norway and Sweden, for some reason, and at least one from Africa. There was one man who taught art at a school in Devonshire, and had been coming down every year.

What was Lanyon like as a teacher?

He was enormously stimulating, even more as a talker than as a teacher in the usual sense. He said he thought painting was terribly difficult and that anybody who did anything was tremendous. He used to take us out in his big car and show us things or details in the local landscape. Once he picked up a handful of sea sand, showed it to me, and said, 'Look, a handful of jewels!' Lanyon was very alive to everything around him. He made us lie on our backs and look up at the sky, and he used to make – as a kind of sketch for his paintings – models out of glass which he would paint. He encouraged us to collect bits of glass from the beach as well, and to stick them together with Bostick as a kind of sculpture. He could get some remarkable effects from that; it was a very good way to study space, which was his main interest.

For instance we'd go to where there was an old tin mine called Botallack, and at Botallack the land came out in a little headland. The way out to it was about half the width of this room and it terrified me. I had to have my eyes shut to be taken across. Anyway, this was to get a feeling of space and what happened. He would say, for instance, 'Look at that seagull. See it is crossing the space in between. That articulates the space for you; otherwise you wouldn't know how far off that was.'

Was the seagull then supposed to be put on the picture surface or its flight marked on the picture surface?

Could be, or you could put a little line which would be the mark of the seagull – your eye-line of the flight of the seagull – but it also meant that if you were looking across one of my big spaces you could articulate this space. By putting a tree or something halfway along you would see how wide it was. He pointed out that Ben Nicholson was very good at this, that he would have this wide landscape with hills and fields and things, and maybe there would be a horse in the middle, the upright thing you needed to show how deep the space was.

Peter Lanyon
(photo: Andrew Lanyon)

Roger Hilton
(photo: Andrew Lanyon)

opposite

The Battery, St Ives

It gave you a completely new way of looking at things.

A new ways of looking at things was what he was trying to do, I think, to stop you from conventional ways of looking, see for yourself and not take on rules. He was very much against rules. He would say, 'You can do anything, remember. You can do anything.'

He had developed a system of 'spiral' space which he had learnt originally from Naum Gabo, the Russian Constructivist sculptor. Gabo had lived and worked in Cornwall, and Peter learned a lot from him. Constructivism really played an important role in forming the St Ives style. I never met Gabo; he had gone to America long before I arrived.

Peter was very attractive personally, a tremendously generous person. He and all his family, including Sheila, his wife, were always friendly to me. So were the other St Ives artists whom I got to know. I knew Roger Hilton pretty well – a difficult man when he had been drinking, but otherwise very charming and intelligent. Bryan Wynter had a particular kind of charm about him, and so had Patrick Hayman, but Hayman stayed a little apart from most of the other artists.

So you got on well with Hilton? Some people found him rather an awkward customer.

Roger used to arrive at my house at the Battery, just on the edge of St Ives – I had left the Redgrave home by then. At this stage he was still an absolutely charming companion, and he would come up for breakfast and talk for hours. He was very well informed about painting, which he had studied in France under Roger Bissière. Roger was also very knowledgeable and up to date about artists' materials and new paint or other mediums, which he would try out and report on. I was not very fond of his painting, but in his later years, when he was often bedridden, he did these very good watercolours and gouaches that are also very witty.

He could be very amusing when he had had a drink or two. There was a famous occasion when, after a session in the pub at Cripplesease, out in the country, he decided to call on Pat Dolan, the painter, who lived a few fields away. The landlord of the Cripplesease was also a farmer, and had a donkey. Roger decided he would ride over to Pat's house; he tried to get up on the donkey, who promptly threw him off. He tried again and again, but the donkey wasn't having it. At last, Roger,on his hands and knees, put his face up against the donkey's and said, 'But you're just a donkey, and you'll always be a bloody donkey!' So then he and a painter called Alan Wood decided to walk to Pat's across country. Going across one field he saw a man working in the adjoining field, and picking up a long stick and brandishing it as a spear, he burst through the hedge with a wild Indian war cry. The man took one look, ran back into his house, and reappeared with a shotgun. Alan vanished into a hedge but Roger walked calmly up to the man and said, 'You seem a very nervous kind of man. Its all right, you know. We are only joking!'

You could always call on him and see his latest work, over a cup of coffee. He was very welcoming that way. There came a time, however, when he got to drinking heavily and could be very unpleasant, so I saw him much less often. A stage sometimes comes in a friendship when the amount of trouble a person causes outweighs the affection you feel for them. It's a pity, but in that kind of situation a decision is more or less forced on you.

When did you move into the Battery, which, I understand, had been built originally as a defence against Napoleonic invasion?

In 1957, I think. I first came down to St Ives in the spring of that year, and I moved into the Battery in the autumn. I rented it for £1 a week from the town council. It was on top of the Island, the grassy hill between Porthmeor beach and the harbour. There are only two buildings on the Island – a little fisherman's church and the Battery, which had been a small fort. It had a gun-emplacement outside, which joins it to the present coastguard's hut.

It was a marvellous place to live. There was just the grass and the rocks and the sea, which crashed on the rocks below the house and slammed down on the roof in stormy weather. The coastguards used to tell me I'd have to go up to it on hands and knees in rough weather, and it was nearly true. There was no electricity up there, so eventually I persuaded the council to let me put up a

Bryan Wynter with his son Billy (photo: Roger Slack)

NWJ at the Tinner's Arms in Zennor, 1958

wind-charger. It charged two car batteries, and I ran the lights, a radio and a record-player off it very successfully. I still had my London studio, but I used it less and less. Occasionally I lent it to friends; for instance, Bryan Wynter borrowed it when he was working for a London show.

You were close to Bryan Wynter?

Quite close, yes. He was very charming and intelligent, with a strong personality, but I don't think this came through in his work. I was interested in his kind of thinking, including scientific areas such as the movement of water. But though he was quite an intense person in himself, I didn't feel that the passion fed into his painting.

Could you describe a typical day in your life in St Ives, when you started living in your own place?

Well, early on Roger might turn up, of course, and he would stay and talk for a while. After that I would probably call on Boots in Island Road, and perhaps do a bit of shopping. Then I would go back and work. There was a lovely studio in the Battery, with big windows and a high barrel roof. And around 1.30 or so I would go down to the Sloop, a pub facing the seafront, and perhaps have half a glass of bitter. Peter only came in the evening, but Roger might be there, or Bryan Wynter, or one of the younger artists. And just one or two of the old fishermen, who were lovely people.

   After lunch I would do some more work, or if it was a nice day I might take the car and go out into the country, to draw perhaps, or to call on Anthony Benjamin, or on Sydney and Nessie Graham. We would all sit outside and talk, and end up at the Gurnard's Head or the Tinner's Arms, where we would probably be joined by other artists. No plans were ever made; it happened as it happened. But the work came first.

During these years – the late fifties – what kind of pictures were you painting? Were they mostly semi-abstract landscapes based on place, in the St Ives manner?

They were, in a sort of way. I took very much to heart what Peter used to say about getting an image from a landscape, doing a lot of drawings and emerging in the end with an image which wasn't pho-tographically true, but true to the spirit of the landscape. He would do a number of drawings from all kinds of angles. He would gradually coalesce them until they produced an image which would convey his feelings of being in a place, of the weather and the atmosphere and the colour, but also the history of the place, and possibly a mythological overlay as well. And I thought that was an exciting idea, and something which I would be able to do. And I did try, but I found it increasingly difficult as time went on. Because I was interested in being close to the actual texture and shapes of the landscape, it was very difficult for me to form an image. I was really trying, I think, to form an image too fast, without having sufficient material matured in my mind, and I wasn't able to mature it in my mind because I would be overwhelmed by the landscape itself.

I produced these large paintings, many of which ended up, in some way, as enormous heads. Another thing I had learned from Peter was the realisation that the sky went all round you and behind you as well. And in attempting to put this and the sea around the land in my picture, I ended up with this kind of head shape. I began to find it difficult to get away from.

They were often almost aerial pictures, map-like in fact. So the influence of Lanyon, and of old Alfred Wallis, was obviously strong then.

Yes, I think it was, extremely strong, though it was a thing I was rather worried about. I wasn't able to twist the landscape around in the way Peter could. I didn't have his spatial gifts. And I think Hilton also influenced me a little. There's a painting I did after a visit to Venice, called *Lagoon*, which was based on the little crumbling palazzos on some of the islands of the lagoon, with black lines suggested by the stakes that used to come out from the islands into the sea as a guide to the fishermen's boats. But, quite unmistakably, it was influenced also by similar shapes in Hilton's work.

Sometimes my pictures were a bit closer to the place itself. There's one called *Levant*, based on an old tin mine or copper mine just down the coast from St Ives, where the copper from the remains of the mine used to leach out into the sea and dye the water pink all around it. It was a mine which went out under the sea, and there had been a terrible disaster when it fell in and a lot of miners were drowned. So the painting was, in one way, almost a picture of the black mine going down, down. It was a kind of death shape, or a tragic shape anyhow. But it did have the pink lines of the sea, and the moorland character of the country round there.

I also did one or two paintings of the local landscape – I think it must have been a little later – which were based on cromlech shapes, or quoits as they call them in Cornwall. And I did figurative paintings with rather Dubuffet-like, graffiti-style figures which were in and part of the landscape. They just arose out of the painting; they weren't predetermined in any sense, but I wanted to develop them more.

During that time, did you have a London gallery, or any regular outlet like that?

I was anxious, from early on in my stay in Cornwall, to get a London gallery. There was a newish one which opened, but didn't last very long, which Peter Lanyon thought I might try. He wrote a letter of introduction and I met the people in London, but they weren't very enthusiastic about the paintings and let it drop. And there was a gallery which a number of St Ives artists showed with called the Lord's Gallery. I showed them some paintings at one time, but again nothing came of it.

You exhibited at a place in Washington in 1959, in a group show with Hilton and Patrick Heron and others. How did that arise?

An American girl arrived in Cornwall and stayed with Boots – her name was Barbara something, I

can't remember. She was connected with a gallery in Washington, and during her stay she assembled a drawing exhibition with works from a number of St Ives artists, including me. That was my first international exhibition, which was of course exciting.

There were quite a lot of those exhibitions. There was one called Twenty Cornish Painters, *I think.*

Yes, there were big shows later in Plymouth and in Cornwall. But a funny thing about the Washington exhibition... The drawings went over there and came back again, and Barbara sent over a little review from the *Washington Post* or something. That appeared to be the end of it, but some years later I sold a picture to the British Arts Council from a show I had in London. I asked the man who bought it if he had ever seen my work before. He said that he had seen it in Washington and had made a note of it. So you can never tell how these things will function.

Obviously by then you were accepted by Hilton and Lanyon as a professional painter of some standing. But who else did you know?

I met John Tunnard. I was taken to see him by Michael Canney at his house at Lamorna Cove, which was a lovely place. It was a beautiful house, full of his paintings; there really were some great beauties there. By that time he'd been almost forgotten, even down in Cornwall, because he was so reclusive. It was quite an effort to see him. But he had seen a painting of mine in Newlyn and liked it, which was one reason why we met.

You must also have known Patrick Heron, who lived nearby in Eagle's Nest at Zennor.

Very much so. Yet somehow we didn't meet very often socially – I think mainly because he and Lanyon had fallen out. He was not a very gregarious man anyway. In those days he was known as much for his art criticism as for his painting. Of course, Patrick suffered from bad asthma, which may have affected his social life there. I remember when he and his wife Delia came to dinner with us they would fall asleep alternately. Finally they would go home at eight o'clock in the morning, saying wasn't it a beautiful morning, and leaving us exhausted.

Patrick Hayman, as you mentioned, was not strictly a St Ives artist. Nevertheless, I have heard you speak highly of both him and his work.

I was very fond of him, though he was only around occasionally. He had lived over in Mevagissey until moving into St Ives. He lived on the outskirts of the town, at a place called Bel-Air. I still think him a very gifted, original painter, and he was a lovely man personally, with an eccentric sense of humour. He moved to Barnes with his wife Barbara, and whenever I was in London I used to go and see them.

And Breon O'Casey?

I'm not sure exactly when Breon appeared, but I knew him when he lived in St Ives. At that time he was a very quiet, shy man who painted small abstracts. He was very busy with local art politics, which didn't interest me much. A little later he got very involved in making jewellery. Breon was always very pleasant to meet, but I had no idea then that he would become such a good friend later in life, when I got to know him much better. By that stage, he and his family were living near Penzance, on the other side of the peninsula.

John Wells is regarded by knowledgeable people as one of the central figures of the St Ives School. Yet he was rather bypassed for years by art fashions.

Johnny Wells was a great favourite of anybody who lived in or near St Ives. He was a wonderful painter, and had been a much-beloved doctor in the Scilly Isles, but you only met him when he came in for parties. At first he was terribly shy and at parties would get very drunk. He was a great friend

John Wells
(photo: Roger Slack)

Denis Mitchell

of Denis Mitchell, and through Denis I got to know what an interesting man he really was, with great charm and a wide knowledge of all the arts. Up to that stage I had not been able to understand why people liked him so much. When Conor and I would return to Cornwall after we left, we always saw him and Denis Mitchell and Breon O'Casey.

And did you know Bernard Leach, the great potter?

Only slightly. I remember dancing with him at parties, and though he must have been into his seventies then, he was very sprightly. He was a very gentle, polite man. Pottery, on the whole – though not Bernard's – rather tended to be looked down on, perhaps because it carried a certain image of beards and sandals. I never met Hamada, his famous partner. He had gone from St Ives by the time I arrived. But we all used Leach pottery on an everyday basis.

Leach's wife Janet was a good potter too, though in a different way. I remember an occasion when Janet had a pot on display in the Penwith, and Bernard came in and started explaining it to somebody. While he was doing that he put his finger in the top, and it stuck. Everybody tried to get it out, but they couldn't. Then Denis Mitchell said: 'You have to decide – either you break the pot and Janet will never forgive you, or you go around for the rest of your life with the pot on your finger.' Finally it was taken off his finger, but I don't know how.

The new American painting was becoming familiar in Britain about the time of your early Cornish years. How did you view it at first? It must have seemed very revolutionary at the time.

Before I went down to St Ives, there was a big American show at the Tate. That was in 1956, I think. I was enormously struck by it, by the scale and colour and the energy. And when I went down to Cornwall, Peter Lanyon had by then exhibited in a New York gallery and he was friendly with a number of the Abstract Expressionists, especially de Kooning and Rothko and a man who was well known at the time but has now fallen out of fashion – Hassall Smith. I think he was a west coast painter and not one of the New York boys. And, of course, Rothko came down to stay with Peter, I think it was about 1958, '59. I met him then and he was enormously impressive. He had the most powerful head, though he was not a big man physically.

Peter and Sheila gave a party for him just before he left. Everybody was dancing, and Rothko came to me across the room to me and said: 'I saw your painting in Newlyn yesterday, and I liked it very much.' I was too flattered and overcome to ask him why he had liked it.

Patrick Heron, in his dual capacity as painter and art critic, must have been one of the first people in Europe, or at least in Britain, to write about the New York School.

He claimed a lot of the credit for recognising the Americans early on, quite rightly too. Patrick Heron was a good critic, and an influential one as well. He got a bee in his bonnet later that English painters had been first in the field, and he himself claimed to have discovered the kind of 'striped' picture which was very much talked about for a time. He said, too, that de Kooning was influenced by Lanyon. There may have been some truth in that, but not much, and in any case I think Heron himself took a good deal from Rothko. He was a great careerist, and I think he had worked out that if it could be proved St Ives art had done certain things first, it would then have greater prestige.

Tony O'Malley must have drifted into your orbit about 1960, or perhaps earlier. I know you were among the first people in St Ives to understand and appreciate his work.

He was staying at Boots Redgrave's then. He had come over from Ireland to work in St Peter's Loft. He didn't come to study, because he was already a mature artist, but he wanted to know other artists and find the right place to work in. So we became very good friends. We were both Celts and had a good deal in common. He thought he had only five years or so to live, and he used to say: 'Nancy, you are a Celtic woman. You must see that I am buried in Ireland,' and I would say: 'Of course, Tony.' That was forty years ago, and he's still going strong.

At that time I did not admire his work greatly, because it was figurative and I thought that any interesting painting had to be abstract, even if it was landscape-based. I respected it, and not much more. But now I like his figurative work best.

Were you at all close to the sculptor Denis Mitchell?

Not terribly at that time. I was quite friendly with him, of course. Denis kept open house in his studio, where you could always go in and have a cup of coffee. But I only became close to him shortly before I left St Ives. Really it was my husband Conor who became so friendly with him. He was married to this Cornish woman who used to put her foot in it regularly – sometimes, I think, deliberately – and Denis used to say 'Jane!' in that deep voice of his. She's still alive, in her nineties. I thought she would collapse when Denis died, since she relied on him so much, but not a bit of it.

Robert Adams – a marvellous sculptor – sometimes came down to St Ives, where he was very much respected as a pioneer and a kind of fellow abstractionist. He was a friend of Tony O'Malley's, but the rest of us didn't meet him often. Later, Conor and I became much more friendly with him, and he even stayed with us in Kinsale when we had moved back to Ireland.

Which artists – I mean living ones – were most admired and influential in Cornwall?

There was a big Matisse exhibition in London at the end of the 1950s, and almost everybody went to see it and was deeply impressed. Picasso seemed irrelevant, really, at that time. Of course he was generally recognised as a truly great painter, but none of us were painting figures then. Practically everybody in St Ives was influenced by Ben Nicholson, and after that by the Abstract Expressionists – Rothko, de Kooning, Kline, Gottlieb. Philip Guston wasn't so well known at that stage. Probably de Kooning was the one most talked about. I've always believed that Bryan Wynter, in particular, was very much influenced by Mark Tobey, who belonged to the older generation of American painters. Tobey did teach for a while at Dartington, and he was also a friend of Bernard Leach. Both men were deeply influenced by the Orient.

The annual exhibitions at the Penwith Gallery in St Ives seem to have been of high quality in those years. You must have shown there, at least occasionally.

No, I didn't in fact. That was because Peter Lanyon had quarrelled with the Penwith committee some years before over their insistence on dividing abstract and figurative work, whereas he thought that good painting was good painting whatever style it was in. So he resigned and began to take an interest in the gallery at Newlyn. He was on the committee and could ensure that there was a wide spectrum of artists shown there. So I used to exhibit in Newlyn; I don't think that the Penwith would have accepted me anyway. There was this very strong, very narrow Hepworth-Nicholson nexus there, and they didn't show much else. They pushed it very much in the direction of abstract art, totally abstract, the kind of thing they were doing themselves, kind of construction-based abstraction.

I don't think you ever met Ben Nicholson. But you must surely have known Barbara Hepworth to some extent.

I did, in fact, meet Nicholson when I first came down to Cornwall, perhaps it was at Boots Redgrave's. At the time he was living quite near, in Salubrious Place. I met him quite often around the place and he would always stop and talk to me. He was a friendly, polite sort of man. Barbara Hepworth I was introduced to a number of times, but she never seemed to remember me from one occasion to the next. So the friendship never did flourish. Ben and Barbara – and when he was gone, just Barbara – had their own court in St Ives. It was rather separate from the rest of us.

Peter was on bad terms with them and didn't speak to either – there was some quarrel from years back, though nobody quite knew what had happened then, as well as the Penwith thing. Nicholson wasn't there for awfully long after I came, because he went off with this German-Swiss woman called Felicitas, and eventually married her. All the same, when he left St Ives, ultimately there was a distinct diminution of energy and quality in the whole society there. Nicholson was not only a very strong personality, he was a kind of benchmark of quality. His kind of craftsmanship made you conscious of having a lot to live up to. And he was such a ruthless professional and perfectionist. If something was not done just the way he wanted it, he would raise hell. Barbara was like that too, of course. Both of them knew exactly what they were doing, and what they wanted.

I remember I shared a room with Felicitas in Boots's place. She had arrived in St Ives saying that she represented Hamburg radio and that she was doing a programme on the St Ives artists. She didn't appear to know an awful lot about modern painting, but on the other hand none of the boys was going to miss out on an opportunity like that. So she was wined and dined, and there was a great deal of manoeuvring to be the last one who had her to dinner. Peter Lanyon thought he had pulled it off, but in fact Ben Nicholson had, and in the end she and Ben disappeared over the horizon to Switzerland.

Who were the younger artists then?

One of them was Robert Law, a minimalist painter who afterwards became quite well known. And there was Anthony Benjamin, who actually lived out in the country, but he'd come into town on occasion. I got to know Anthony very well, and his wife Stella. They were the most charming-look-

NWJ with Anthony
Benjamin, Cripplesease,
1958

NWJ and WS Graham,
1958 (photo: Michael Snow)

ing young couple you could see. Both of them wore pale-coloured clothes – lots of mauves and pinks
and things like that – and they had a huge lurcher dog, and often went about in bare feet. I know it
sounds awfully hippy – it was awfully hippy – but somehow they carried it off with such grace.
Anthony became a great friend of mine, and I was his confidante when his marriage broke up; he
used to pour it all out to me.

Alan Lowndes would sometimes be there. Terry Frost was away most of the time and I didn't
see him very often. He worked very hard and he had a lot of young children. I think he and Cath,
his wife, had a job to cope with the situation and to make both ends meet.

Who were the writers there? Cornwall always had the reputation for attracting poets and novelists.

Well, WS – Sydney – Graham, the Scottish poet, used to come into St Ives from Gurnard's Head,
where he lived in this isolated house, to do a bit of shopping or just to see people. After knowing
him for a while, I became deeply involved with him. I didn't feel guilty about it because I knew that
he and his wife Nessie had an open marriage anyway, and she had affairs too. I knew also that she
knew about it, but it was never mentioned between us. My common sense told me there was no
future in it, because he and Nessie basically cared only for one another. All the same, I couldn't help
hoping that something would happen later on.

And was that based mainly on the excitement of his poetry?

I think it was, yes. He was a very clever man, and when he wasn't too drunk to be coherent, he was
an interesting conversationalist. And he was very attractive when he was younger. He sang too; he

was a good singer. Sydney was particularly interesting on what you might call the philosophy of art, on what art was basically about. Really, right up to the time I met Conor we were still kind of half-involved, you know. And we remained very good friends, all three of us, Nessie as well.

He believed that he knew about painting, but I think that in reality he hadn't much feeling for it.

That's right. Peter used to say that writers in general didn't have any plastic feeling at all. I think that's very true; they don't, as a rule. The visual artist is much more involved with the material aspect of the world. He gets his hands dirty.

Sydney at that time would have been involved with Roger Hilton's wife, wouldn't he?

Yes, with Ruth Hilton. She wasn't often there. She was a musician, and Roger's first wife. He was married twice.

Francis Bacon used to visit Cornwall in the early sixties. Did you have any contact with him?

Francis was down for some months, and I got to be very friendly with him. Boots and Peter and the others all knew him from Soho, though I didn't. He was very much a big-city person, but he had taken one of those large studios over Porthmeor Beach to get away from London for a while and have a part-time place to work in for an exhibition. He had just moved to the Marlborough Gallery from the Hanover. Francis stayed originally with John Milne, and then afterwards he had a flat of his own right on the harbour in St Ives. I first met him, I think, because John Milne came to ask me if I would take him and Francis and his boyfriend into Falmouth. John didn't have a car, and he thought I might like to meet Bacon anyway. This would have been about 1960 I should think.

    Francis was marvellous company, and very witty. He used to come up to the Battery and sit around and have a cup of tea. He was a splendid talker, very interesting on art, and very forthright about it too. He thought, for instance, that a tremendous lot of the art that was being done was insufficiently personal, and that people were making art out of art, rather than trying to express their own sensations and experiences. He usually had his boyfriend with him. Ron was his name, and he was generally quiet and inoffensive when he wasn't high on amphetamines.

In the Sloop, St Ives, c.1960; from left: Karl Weschke, Nancy Wynne-Jones, WS Graham, Nessie Graham, the sculptor Brian Wall, and the painter Michael Snow

And did Bacon show any interest in your painting?

Not tremendously. He wasn't really interested in anyone else's work, but he was encouraging. We went to parties and events together, and I remember one time – admittedly after a party, when we were all pretty drunk – he and I were arm in arm, and we made plans to go to Greece together. It never came off though.

I remember once in the Sloop, Roger Hilton had been drinking and called out to Francis: 'If you come up to my studio one of these days, I can give you lessons in how to paint.' Bacon replied like a flash: 'How kind of you, darling, I only wish I could give you some of my genius.'

Francis used to have these huge canvases sent down to him, and he might only paint on one corner of them. At other times he worked on boards which he would cut up and leave bits of them lying around the studio. Tony O'Malley took over that studio after him, and he painted on the other sides of a number of them, so that some of Tony's pictures have half a Bacon on the reverse side.

Did he try to involve you in his life in London?

No, though after he went back to London I used to meet him occasionally, at some pub or other, very often the French Pub in Soho. And gradually it became more and more difficult to see him, perhaps because his life grew more extreme and he spent a lot of time in the East End with quite violent characters. He believed that criminals were the only really free people, because they had no inhibitions in any direction. That was why he found their company interesting, or one of the reasons anyway.

Bacon had two basic maxims, I remember. The first was that you should know all art that has been done before you. The second was don't be afraid to make a fool of yourself.

Can you pinpoint the years when certain paintings of yours were created? Or are all those St Ives years, for you, just a single period?

It is actually a single period for me. I was still grappling with this idea of painting a whole area of country rather than an individual viewpoint, or even a multiple viewpoint, of a particular place. I was still attempting to do that and because – as I mentioned already – these paintings often tended to come out like heads, I became interested in the idea of making them shape themselves into whole figures, partly through the very texture of my paint. I remember one landscape of Portugal which had taken on a head-like form that was the image of Roger Hilton, and I did another landscape which turned into a picture of Peter Lanyon, but could also be seen as a kind of cliff. That was painted in 1959.

Did he like it when he saw it?

Fairly well, yes. Sheila Lanyon didn't like it at all, however, because it made him look rather moon-faced, so she thought. And so this developed into these other, graffiti-like figures – again, rather like Dubuffet, though I don't know if I had seen Dubuffet's work at this time.

Did you feel you were developing or that you had a basic problem?

I didn't feel I had a problem, no. I thought they were all more or less temporary kinds of things. I did believe I was developing, though I didn't feel that I was 'there' compared with the other St Ives

painters – Lanyon, Wynter, Hilton, even Patrick Heron. I did consider then that they were more skilled than I was. But I still had total faith in my essential worth as a painter.

So up to the time you moved to Trevaylor, near Penzance, in 1962, you were wholly a landscape artist – at least in your own particular sense?

Yes, I was, and that happened in St Ives, which I suppose developed out of the landscapes I had done from that visit to Portugal. Before that, I had been a lot more abstract in a different kind of way – much more formal, or formalised.

And did you draw a lot in this period, as well as paint?

I did. This was probably from Peter Lanyon's example. He used to go out and draw around the countryside with black conté crayon, and I started to do this and found it suited me very well. So I would go out and draw the landscape, sometimes with Tony O'Malley. We went to Botallack mine together once, and Tony was very excited to discover that in part of the old workings there were chimneys full of beautiful black soot. He thought this would be wonderful to paint and draw with, and he collected a whole lot for both of us. We mixed it with linseed, and it did make the most beautiful black. It was lovely to use too. You felt you were using what was at hand, what was part of the country, and part of the whole history of the country too.

In painting and drawing did you have what Cézanne would call a motif? Or did you do a gener-alised, Lanyonesque version of the landscape?

More of a generalised thing, except that I never really grasped Lanyon's spatial talents.

To whom did you talk about painting at that time?

I talked a lot to Sydney Graham, who was very interested in visual art. His understanding of it was a bit partial, but he was interested in the creative act in itself. I talked too to Karl Weschke, a painter with whom I was friendly, and to Peter, of course. I suppose, in retrospect, a little to all the artists.

Denis Mitchell I used to talk to as well. And very often in the pub, in the evening, a group of us would get on to discussing art, and I would contribute – though, out of shyness, not a tremendous amount.

You had your first London show in 1962. How exactly did that happen?

It happened really through my Polish friend, Olga Karchevskaya. She came down to St Ives once or twice – she stayed with Boots on Island Road – and she loved the whole atmosphere of St Ives. She was always interested in my painting, and she became friendly with a man named Denis Bowen, who ran a London gallery called the New Vision Centre. I went up and showed him works of mine, and he was enthusiastic and offered me a joint exhibition with Olga.

By 1962 I had come to a rather transitional stage. I did these half-figurative things, and I also did a number of paintings which were figurative, but with birds and animals rather than people. These were quite solidly painted, but flat and brilliantly coloured. I don't have any of them today. I think later they were destroyed by damp.

I sold one or two pictures from the exhibition, one of them – as a kind of family thing, I suppose – to Peter Scott, a cousin of my mother's. At that time he was head of Provincial Insurance, and apparently the painting – a landscape – still hangs in the boardroom of the firm. There was a review of the show in *Art News*, which was reasonably enthusiastic.

Who else showed at the New Vision?

Some quite well-known people. Fontana showed there once or twice, I think, and so did Paul Jenkins and Robert Goodenough, both of whom were American. Jenkins was very well known at the time, in fact. And Michael Rothenstein and Bill Gear – William Gear – exhibited there too.

Olga went on to Nîmes and started an art school there, rather along the lines of St Peter's Loft. Boots Redgrave was supposed to go in with her but somehow didn't in the end, but Olga went ahead anyway and made a great success of it.

During all this, was your contact with Lanyon as strong as ever?

It was, but I didn't see him as often as before. As he progressively became better known he had a number of exhibitions abroad, particularly in America – he had a gallery in New York – and in Zurich, which was a great place at the time for people to show in. He also went on lecture tours and he was still teaching at Corsham school, so he wasn't at home in St Ives a tremendous lot, but when he was I should think we were as friendly as ever. I used to go and see him in his studio quite often.

Just what, above all, did St Ives give you apart from high-quality, sympathetic colleagues and a feeling for finish and fine craftsmanship? Did Lanyon, for instance, give you any special tuition in the use of oils?

Yes, he did in fact. I would even say I learned basic craftsmanship from him. He thought me how to put on size and to prepare the ground for wood panels, among other things. And I think it was from him that I acquired the habit of painting with very big brushes – almost like whitewash brushes. He painted in oils which he ground himself. I learned how to do that, and I used to buy the powder colour from a merchant called Cornelison and grind them myself. And, of course, there was the fashion – mainly American – to paint only on six-by-four boards.

But Lanyon did not attempt to form your style?

He encouraged you to follow your own instincts, to feel that every thing was possible and that you should try anything.

And your main subject and interest was still landscape?

Yes, it was. And because Lanyon painted a whole area or region rather than once specific place, I tried for a time to do the same. But in the end, it really did not suit me and I had to make other decisions. You see, I am much more interested in painting what is before my eyes. That is the chief reason why I almost always imply the horizon line, since that is what you see in front of you. For me, it is much more honest to use one.

Did the sea around Cornwall offer you much?

Not immensely. On a personal level it did, no doubt. I got to love it and I don't like being far away from the sea, but I don't paint it often. I don't like being in boats, for instance. I am very much a landswoman.

And the famous St Ives light?

Yes, that was extraordinary. It derived from the sea, of course. West Penwith – that is to say, the peninsula stretching down to Land's End – is almost an island. So the light is refracted from the sides and it is very brilliant; it has that northern quality. But it also made things difficult, in a way. You could do a picture down there which was tonally perfect, yet when you brought it up to London it might look simply dark, the difference in light was so great.

Do you think that it encouraged a certain black-and-white tonality?

It's possible. But I was never drawn to the black-and-white spectrum. People like William Scott, for example, obviously were.

It seems to me that there is almost a Continental tonality in your work at times; of course, you have painted in a number of European countries, including France. Certainly you do not have a typically English palette. It's not typical of Irish painting either, which tends to be misty – Patrick Collins' work, for instance.

Here in Ireland I find that people generally prefer the colours they are most used to – greens, blues, greys. I notice that tendency in their reactions to my own pictures, for instance. I tend myself to go more for warm colours, such as ochres and reds.

During your Cornish years, you made at least one visit to Italy. Did that affect your palette and your feeling for light very deeply?

Yes, I made a number of visits – perhaps seven or eight altogether. First of all, I had gone to Venice to study Tintoretto, a visit I've described already. Of course I was amazed by the richness of Italy and how every little town church had a good painting in it. I was particularly entranced by Giotto and Masaccio, and by Mantegna, and of course Piero della Francesca, who became my very favourite painter. But I think it had a bad influence on my work because I got very interested in the colours of frescoes such as Giotto's, which made my tonality too pale. I began trying to use these flat pale colours which have such resonance and look so good in Italian light, but which would never look right in St Ives. Also, the simplicity of forms did not suit me, though I tried to emulate them.

The Italian light, of course, was a revelation, and I fell in love with the Mediterranean. Later, I fell equally in love with the south of France. And the beauty of the paintings which you might come across even in tiny villages, the richness of it all... But I am not really a classical painter, I realise now, much more of a Romantic.

How much does Constable, for instance, mean to you? I mention him as an obvious representative of English Romanticism in painting, and even of the northern European landscape sensibility in general.

I now love and admire Constable very much. But at that time I was not enormously interested in the art of the past, apart from what I discovered for myself in Italy. Constable was too familiar to me; it took me years to see him with fresh eyes.

Where did you exhibit in Cornwall, apart, that is, from the group shows in Newlyn?

I did not have any solo exhibitions in Cornwall. But in 1963 Denis Bowen organised an exhibition in Florence for me, at a place called the Galleria Numero. I still don't understand how anyone could find that gallery – in a narrow little street at the back of a courtyard, and on the first floor. Of course, I didn't sell anything there. The paintings themselves were on mythological subjects, mostly Greek. I painted a whole series of those, and pictures on Celtic myths as well. But finally that vein ran out on me, too. In any case, most of these works were later destroyed by damp when they were stored in the stables of Trevaylor, the big country house I lived in from 1962 to 1972.

Did the Cornish landscape still appeal to you very strongly?

Yes, I felt an intimacy with it. But I also found it difficult to handle, and I never quite managed to make relevant images of it in the way I wanted. There was something about it – the sea, the kind of light – which enormously attracted me, but it was not really for me, in the end.

I loved Cornwall. I still do, and I dream about it a lot. In a way I still feel it to be my own country. It offered such an excellent life for artists for one thing, and it was an unstructured life, one which was not planned. You just wandered into someone's studio, where you were either welcomed or asked to come back in the afternoon. Or you might sit all day on the cliffs somewhere, with somebody sympathetic. It was not like. 'I'll meet you for tea next Friday' or that kind of thing.

And the pub life was stimulating as well, of course.

Yes, there was always that too. At the end of the day's work everybody would go down from their studios or other workplaces and congregate in the Sloop or the Castle. You knew everyone who came in, whether it was the local farmers or the artists themselves. Then there was the Tinner's Arms in Zennor, about five miles out, and a bit further out again, the Gurnard's Head. The landlord at the Gurnard, Jimmy Goodman, loved the artists and would keep you there all night sometimes. He would throw out people he didn't want at closing time, and you could stay behind for as long as you liked. That could mean a mixture of local farmers who were friends of his, and the artists.

I remember they had table skittles in the Sloop, and some of the fishermen were very good at that. One of them, old Dickie, had worked on a big yacht, and there was Tommy who was the pilot for Hayle, just across the bay from St Ives, and the other was a local fisherman. I would come down from the Battery, and they would invite me to join them at one of these long tables. Then if one of my artist friends appeared, they would quietly slip away. They were so well-mannered.

The barmaid in the Sloop, Margaret, had learned to lip-read, and you would see her suddenly burst into hysterical giggles at something she had seen at the other end of the room. All the artists used to gather on Saturdays at lunchtime, and we would often take our drinks outside if it was warm enough.

Nearly every Saturday night there was a party somewhere. It was the easiest thing to organise one: you just went into the Sloop, said 'party in the Battery tonight', and everyone there would turn up, bottle in hand. In St Ives everybody knew everybody; that was what I found so charming. That included the local fishermen as well as the farmers. John Berryman and Willy Craze would have parties in their big stone barns, and you would walk down the lanes to them by starlight. It was a marvellous mixture of city sophistication and country living.

In spite of working in one's studio, it was an outdoor kind of life. You tended more often than not to sit outside the pub or outside somebody's house. Heading down to Sydney Graham's house on Gurnard's Head you would walk along this path lined with gorse, and arrive at this place poised above the sea, with the old tin mines just below, and the black cliffs covered with sea pinks and screaming seagulls.

I remember one afternoon I had walked from there up to the Gurnard's Head pub with Sydney and Robert Brennan. Most of the young artists in St Ives got evening jobs washing up or as waiters in order to be able to paint during the day. Robert had got a job as the Zennor postman, and the Grahams' house was the last on his round, which he covered on a bicycle. It was a lovely day, and sitting in the pub, looking at a huge pair of buffalo horns which Jimmy had mounted on the wall, Sydney thought it would be fun to have a bullfight in the car park. So we fixed the horns onto the handlebars of Robert's bike. Daphne lent us her red petticoat, and we were away. Sydney danced around shouting 'Toro! Toro!, and Robert charged him at top speed on his bicycle. They both fell around of course, but nobody was hurt and it was great fun. We were all helpless with laughter. Unfortunately one of the local biddies was spying from her very distant window, and poor Robert lost his job for 'endangering Government property'.

No doubt there were cliques and factions?

There were, of course. It was an odd thing how these divisions – some of them deep – existed between Lanyon and Nicholson, or between Lanyon and Heron. Of course, Lanyon could be truculent and uneasy with his peers. But there was a strong sense of comradeship too. We all banded together against outsiders, and if anybody was in trouble we all rallied around.

———

St Ives and Trevaylor

Dawn Dance
1965, air-brush enamel on canvas, 127 × 102 cm (50 × 40 in)

Trevaylor Road
1965, egg tempera on paper, 37 × 32 cm (14.5 × 12.5 in)

Shield Fields
1965, egg tempera on paper, 37 × 55 cm (14.5 × 21.5 in)

Carn Brea
1965, oil on canvas, 51 × 76 cm (20 × 30 in)

The Red Path
1966, oil on canvas, 56 × 46 cm (22 × 18 in)

Yellow Chûn
1965, egg tempera on paper, 35 × 50 cm (13.75 × 19.75 in)

Summer Road
1965, egg tempera on paper, 35 × 50 cm (13.75 × 19.75 in)

Mas Thibert, Noon
1966, oil pastel on paper, 28 × 23 cm (11 × 9 in)

Salier Vineyard
1966, oil pastel on paper, 23 × 28 cm (9 × 11 in)

Telemachus at Pylos
1967, acrylic on canvas, 168 x 122 cm (66 x 48 in)

Cregennan Lovers with Clock
1971, acrylic on canvas, 76 x 63.5 cm (30 x 25 in)

August Yard
1971, acrylic on canvas, 102 × 63.5 cm (40 × 25 in)

Orphic Landscape
1970, oil on canvas, 76 × 102 cm (30 × 40 in)

III

1962–1972: move to Trevaylor; Lanyon's death; marriage

In 1962 you moved to Trevaylor, a large country house a few miles outside Penzance. After the close, almost communal lifestyle of St Ives, it must have been quite a major change.

I moved from the Battery mainly because St Ives was becoming more and more crowded with tourists, especially in the summer season. At that time cars were allowed to park on the Island, and at times they were almost up to my door. A stream of visitors just trooped along a path past my house and looked in at the windows, or sat on a seat just outside, so I had no real privacy any longer. At night it was rather frightening, because you would suddenly hear this muttering in the dark just under your window, and the Battery was quite isolated. So I thought I should like to live somewhere just outside St Ives, like Bryan Wynter, who lived on top of a moor.

Boots Redgrave also thought she would like to move into the country and run an art school there, because St Peter's Loft was faltering. Peter wasn't often there now, and Bill Redgrave spent more and more time in London, while Terry Frost had this teaching job in Reading. And so we decided we'd buy a biggish place together, and I would live in part of it and she would run a residential school in the other half and get local artists to come in and teach.

I began looking around then for a place in the neighbourhood which might suit both of us. One day Jimmy Goodman rang up and told me that 'old Mrs Brooke Bond Tea' had just died and had no near relatives. I didn't know her, or who she was, but she had left this beautiful Georgian-style house in Gulval, near Penzance, overlooking Mounts Bay, which was to be sold. Jimmy told me I should get in touch with solicitors called Poole. Mr Poole was very surprised when I contacted him, because it wasn't generally known that the house – which was called Trevaylor – was about to be sold, but he arranged for me to see it. Boots and I went down to have a look at it, and it was the most beautiful place – largely 18th century but dating back to Elizabethan times in places. It was built of golden Cornish granite, and it was spacious and peaceful and had ten acres of garden and woodland, including two walled gardens. There was also a superb view over St Michael's Mount, out to sea. Of course we fell completely in love with it, and I rang Mr Poole and asked him the price. He hadn't really thought about it, but he rang me back the next day and said 'ten thousand'. So I said at once 'right, done'. I thought it was a tremendous bargain, and I still think it was too.

Trevaylor had lots of old buildings and outhouses, and even a studio, because Mrs Brooke

Trevaylor from the air, c.1968 (photo: Skyviews Aerial Archives)

97

Bond Tea had done a bit of painting herself. She was called that because she owned Brooke Bond Tea – she was really a Miss Hooper. I rented half of it to Boots Redgrave, who was always going to start her art school, but in the end she never did. She used to have her in-lodgers there, such as Tony O'Malley. He and Bill Featherstone, a big, red-bearded Canadian sculptor, both had studios in the outbuildings. There were various other artists, too, who would appear from time to time. It worked very well for a few years, but things began to get more difficult, mainly because my relations with Boots were becoming strained. Then I married Conor Fallon in 1966, and shortly after that we took over the whole of the house, while Boots moved to Nancledra.

When I first moved out to Trevaylor, Sydney Graham and Nessie were still living in the old coastguard house on Gurnard's Head, right down on the cliff. It was a fine building and quite large, but primitive – an outdoor loo and all that. The Grahams weren't ones for making a home, and they had no income anyway. Nessie became ill. I can't quite remember with what, but she always had a dicky heart. Sydney came to stay with me while she was in hospital, and then later she came too while she recuperated. After they'd been a while in Trevaylor they really didn't want to go back to their coastguard station. So I bought what was called the 'Little House', which had once been the lodge to Trevaylor and was just across the road from it, and moved them into that.

They lived there more or less until I got married – very happily, I think – and they used to come over and have their evening meal with me. For some reason they didn't like the name 'Little House' and changed it to Woodfield. There was a lovely little wood directly behind it, and a stream ran through it. Since they had no money, I decided to give them a small weekly income to keep them going, and I arranged for it to be sent down from London so they wouldn't know who it was from. I think they rather fancied it was from TS Eliot, who had helped Sydney over the years.

Was that when Sydney Graham and Tony O'Malley became friends?

No, Tony had been friendly with Sydney for some time, because I often brought him down to the coastguard station. I used to go there every Sunday with a joint of meat and a bottle of whiskey. Sydney, who was a good cook in a rough-and-ready way, used to cook an absolutely delicious pot roast, and we'd drink the whiskey while we waited for it.

And your chosen pubs were still the Gurnard's Head and the Tinner's Arms, I take it. But you also

Matt and Mirren in the Sportsman, yes. They were very nice. But my favourite pub was always the Gurnard's Head. It was an isolated place, but Jimmy and Daphne Goodman were very friendly people and always terribly interested in the artists. They used to have the most ferocious fights together in the kitchen, which was just around from the bar. Sometimes they would invite me to lunch there. Daphne was a very good cook.

But leaving pubs aside for the moment, there were marvellous walks all around Trevaylor, through the woods and over the fields. The wild flowers were wonderful, including primroses, bluebells; the woods were full of them. We were on the edge of the moorland country, where the old tin mines are, and Ding Dong mine was just a mile away. We used to to go there for picnics, and even for barbecues. Trevaylor also stood on the edge of very ancient country, and what the Cornish call a quoit – in Ireland it's called a dolmen – was quite close. I used to walk up there a lot with Tony O'Malley and we took rubbings of the stone, which turned out to have a similar pattern to stones in Ireland. Cornwall is a very ancient country, full of Bronze Age and Neolithic remains. The climate was very warm and gentle, but we used to get whole days of thick sea fogs when almost everything was blotted out.

Trevaylor was also beautifully placed, on the edge of the high moors. I have never seen such a marvellous colour as the deep blue of the summer sea in Cornwall, edged by the black cliffs. On the south side it was semi-tropical, and we could grow tree-ferns and even palms in the garden. There was a Chilean fire tree there too. The garden was famous, and had once been open to the public, well before my time. We inherited the gardener, Stephen May, who was a marvellous man, and his wife Betty, who looked after the house for us. There was a revolving summerhouse, where sometimes we used to sit out and have breakfast, and a sundial on the lawn. And with fourteen bedrooms, a number of people could live there together and also have privacy.

There was a special atmosphere; it was a very happy kind of house. The big windows let in plenty of light, and there was lots of space for people to get away from one another. And then, the garden melted away into other landscape vistas. Miss Hooper had placed little seats through the woods, with tables in front of them, so you could sit and do drawings. Or you could wander through masses of camellias and then through fields of lupins. The house also had this large walled garden,

NWJ in her studio at
Trevaylor, 1965
(photo: Andrew Lanyon)

and I and my mother-in-law used to freeze masses of peas and beans and raspberries. Trevaylor is now an old people's home.

Did your painting change very much after your move there?

Yes, because by then I was dissatisfied with what I had done before. I felt that it wasn't sufficiently personal, that it was too much influenced by Lanyon and the nature-based abstraction of St Ives. Although I still liked that, I couldn't find my own way into it, and so I was trying to do paintings based on an area of landscape rather than on the individual aspect of the eye – you know, what the eye actually saw. I still wasn't able to make anything out of that; I was still too overwhelmed by the landscape to impose my own vision on it or to make a direct relationship with it.

I went with the Grahams to Greece, and a large part of that holiday – the most important part – was spent in Crete. I only did a few drawings there, but when I came back I did a number of abstract paintings, based on my memories of Crete, with a spray gun. A lot of these were quite big paintings, which were shown at the New Vision Centre in 1965. I had got a lot of tins of car enamel, and I found you could do all sorts of things with these and the spray gun. It was extremely linear in technique, as well as being able to cover large flat areas, and the colours were very clear. But the spray paintings weren't any sort of success. They had good reviews, but no sales. I think I sold just one of them. And almost immediately after that I stopped spray-painting, because I couldn't think of anything else to do with it except to repeat myself.

I also painted a good deal in egg tempera, from about 1965 – not big abstract or semi-abstract pictures, but smaller, more realistic ones. I loved the egg-tempera colours, which had great depth and resonance, but I found some of them, especially the blacks, were susceptible to a kind of fungus, very common in Cornwall because of the climate. So I had to give up using them in the end.

I was almost in despair about what to do next, about how to proceed from there at all. The odd thing was, all the time I had been doing watercolours and small things in pastels, and so on, but because I was fixated on the idea of abstract painting, I hadn't considered these as being in any way important. They were just something I enjoyed doing, for their own sake.

Do you think that attitude went back to your early conviction – nourished by Herbert Read – that modern painting had to be abstract?

I think it did. I hadn't ever really considered up till then how painters arrived at abstraction, as I said earlier. I sort of felt that it sprang fully formed from their heads. But also, after the war, one rather tended to keep away from things which were too hurtful, I suppose. The world had turned out to be a very hurtful place for a while, and it took time for that consciousness to heal. And in any case I was under the influence of the whole St Ives ethos, which was basically abstract.

How did this ethos affect a man like Tony O'Malley, for instance?

Tony arrived in St Ives as a realistic painter, an excellent one in his own, slightly expressionist way. He was generally considered to be a totally made, mature artist; there wasn't any question that he came for instruction or anything. But equally, his painting wasn't of great interest to many people there. It was generally considered to be old-fashioned and something which had been done before. He was quite hurt by this attitude, and when he came to live in Trevaylor in 1962 it gave him the opportunity to change his style to abstract painting – something he could do more or less in privacy, without having to expose himself.

He wasn't enormously influenced as a painter by Lanyon, although I think he admired Lanyon's work. But as he said, Peter gave you the feeling you could do anything. As individuals, however, they were never very close.

Was he close to Hilton, then, or to Terry Frost?

Friendly with Hilton, I should say, but not close. I don't know if he was ever very close to any of them really, though he and Bryan Wynter were good friends. Patrick Heron used to ask him to Eagle's Nest for dinner, I remember, and he stayed there at times. Who was he close to? I suppose to Alan Lowndes, who was also a non-abstract painter, and they had a rather similar sense of humour. And Sydney Graham he was close to as well. Sydney was a word man, and Tony was always very interested in words and poetry.

Most of the St Ives artists seem to have had some interest in poetry. Bryan Wynter was highly informed about it, so I am told.

Absolutely, they were generally very interested in poetry. And they all had a great admiration for Sydney Graham. He was a kind of icon poet for them, you know, and they all respected him very much.

And had you more or less lost contact with Hilton by this time?

I had, but I used to see him occasionally. Sometimes he'd come over to see Sydney. He would hire a taxi, and they would go off somewhere together. But after a time they would get so drunk and rowdy that none of the taximen would take them, so Roger would try to get lifts from people.

He rang me one night and said he was up in Georgia with his small boy, and it was dreary and could they possibly come down and spend the night with me? This was about one o'clock in the morning, and he was obviously very drunk, so I said no. I thought to myself I really couldn't bear it at that hour. Ages afterwards he told me he was there alone with his small son, and he felt as if he were about to kill himself and was afraid for the child, and that was why he had rung me. That made me feel awful, which, knowing Roger, was quite probably his intention.

Lanyon's death in 1964 was an enormous blow to St Ives art and to art in general. Can you describe the effect it had on you, in particular?

It was absolutely devastating, because apart from his big, strong, warm personality, he more or less epitomised the whole Cornish idyll for me. The Cornish experience was exemplified in Lanyon, and he was the rock and the energy of the whole place. And he was also the one who exemplified the whole going-forward-into, pushing-into, area of modern art, where we all felt we were going, but he was the one who definitely was. With his death a whole direction had gone for me, and I had lost my exemplar, in a sense.

He was your critic as well, a voice you could depend on.

Exactly, he was. Although, I'm bound to say that by that time, even though I respected him so much, I didn't find his judgement or advice particularly helpful any more. In the end, you find that you are alone with your work and that nobody can tell you absolutely what to do. Any suggestions people may make to you are never wholly to the point.

You first met Conor Fallon in Wales in 1964.

We met through Tony O'Malley. He was an old friend of Padraic Fallon, the poet, and had known the family and all six sons since they were boys. When Tony moved from Ireland to Cornwall – on the advice of Padraic Fallon, who had said on Tony's retirement from the bank through ill-health, 'Here is your chance to live with other painters' – one or other of the sons used to come to visit him each year.

In 1964 it was Conor who came, and he stayed in Trevaylor. Conor was painting, not sculpting in those days, and was anxious to meet Peter Lanyon. I rang Peter's wife Sheila to arrange it, to be told by a frightened Sheila that Peter had had a gliding accident, and was in hospital. A day or so later he was dead. Everyone was shocked and grieved, and held a loud sort of wake for him, drinking whiskey and singing, but all I could do was sit quietly in a corner and cry. I had dearly loved him, and he was such an important part of my life. Conor was the only person who seemed to understand this.

Conor went back to Ireland, and in the autumn I wrote to him inviting him to come to my opening in London in February. I thought if he didn't come it would break my heart. But he did come, and that was when we came together. I went to visit him in Dublin, he came up to Wales to meet my parents, his parents came to Trevaylor, letters flew to and fro. We were married in Arthog, beside Penmaenucha, in the spring of 1966 on Grand National day. My father brought the television into the reception, and the only person who chose the winner was the saintly old canon who married us.

Our honeymoon was in France, in Arles and St Remy, because of van Gogh. We used to buy a picnic every day of a baguette, apples, cheese, and a bottle of wine and drive out into the Camargue to draw. The Camargue was unspoilt in those days. People were working in the fields, and there were marvellous birds, great flocks of flamingoes on the *étangs*. Sometimes we would see the famous black bulls or the white horses. It was magical. Since those days we have spent a lot of time in France; we both love it very much. Nearly all my art influences, apart from Lanyon and the Abstract Expressionists, have been from French painting – Bonnard, Monet, Segonzac and Hayden – most of all Bonnard perhaps. I find the study in his paintings of what your eye actually sees, of how peripheral things are out of focus, how colours shift, immensely interesting. In St Ives, of

Conor Fallon at Crankan,
Penzance, 1966

NWJ with the six Fallon
brothers at Trinity College,
Dublin, 1966;
from left (in strict order of
age): Garrett, Brian, Conor,
Niall, Ivan and Padraic

course, people had been reared almost entirely on French art.

People sometimes ask me if it is difficult for two artists to be married to each other, but we have never found it so. On the contrary, I rely immensely on knowing that Conor is working near me, and I believe he feels the same way. When we came home to Cornwall, I started off on a new expressionist phase, I think through drawing in the Camargue and Conor's influence, because at that time he was painting rather than sculpting. Some people might think of his painting as naturalistic, but anyway he wasn't abstract, although well aware of what was going on. We both of us did hundreds of drawings in Provence, a lot in oil pastels, and I now did paintings from those.

We rented a small farmhouse at Crankan while we arranged for our tenants in Trevaylor to leave. This little house was quite close to Trevaylor, and I did a lot of work there, or in the fields around. These pictures, which were not big, were quite Expressionist in style and not at all abstract. I also drew much more out of doors, mostly in black-and-white using conté crayon – again, probably Lanyon's influence. It was a good way of expressing the big rhythms of the Cornish country and the swell of the hills.

We finally moved into Trevaylor, I think, in January 1967. I had been thinking a great deal about possible subjects to paint, and resurrected my old love of Greek and Celtic mythology, which always lay deep in my imagination. I now had a big studio again, and I did a series of large paintings on these themes. One was of the *Singing Head of Bran*, and others were of classical Greek subjects – Telemachus, for instance, and the Argonauts. Another was called *Mourning for Hector*. I also did some paintings based on the writings of Bulgakov, which I had just discovered and very much admired. And another again was of the reddleman, a subject out of Hardy's novel *The Return of the Native*.

I think it was about this time, too, that I discovered Beckmann and was immensely excited by him, especially his treatment of myth. It opened up to me the whole of German painting, and particularly German Expressionism, which I hadn't really thought of much before, although I already owned a big book on Nolde, I remember.

Your husband, who has a special insight into your work, believes that your early Portuguese paintings link up crucially with the small egg-tempera works of the mid-sixties, and that in these you had arrived at a great deal of what your painting is now. A kind of underground development, if I may put it that way.

I think, looking back, that I had arrived in that sense, but I didn't recognise it, because I had thought of those as once-off things rather than as part of my mainstream development. They had this combination – which I had been hoping for all the time – of the eye and the mind and the place. But as I said, I didn't actually recognise the fact. I thought, you know, there was not enough brain, enough intellect in it to satisfy me.

So it seems that you were still intent on imposing a certain kind of intellectual content on your painting at that time?

Yes, I think I was.

And that isn't from Peter Lanyon or Roger Hilton or any of these people. According to Conor, it's more from Herbert Read.

It's from Herbert Read, yes, and my fascination with his ideas way back. That's true.

When you went back to Trevaylor early in 1967, you were painting those big mythic pictures. They

Nancy Wynne-Jones
Le Paradis, Camargue
1966, oil pastel on paper,
23 × 28 cm (9 × 11 in)

opposite

Nancy Wynne-Jones and
Conor Fallon on their
wedding day at
Penmaenucha, Wales, 1966

NWJ drawing on her
honeymoon in the
Camargue, 1966

formed the main body of your 1970 exhibition at the Project Arts Centre in Dublin, presumably.

Yes, they did. When Conor's parents arrived to live in Cornwall in 1967 I was still painting the big mythological pictures, because my father-in-law was very interested in my Bran paintings. He was a poet, of course, and seriously interested in myth. But gradually I came to the end of those, and that was very discouraging for me. And I even gave up exhibiting at all. I didn't show in Newlyn or anywhere. But Michael Byrne, an Irish painter who had stayed with us in Trevaylor and was an old friend of Conor's, suggested that I should have a show at the Project Arts Centre and arranged it for me. By that time my gallery in London had folded.

But in that show you also had a lot of smaller works in oil pastel, possibly as many as fifty. You had mounted them and put them behind cellophane, but they were unframed.

They were unframed, just as in a portfolio. It made them easier to look at and buy. And they all sold – everything in that medium, in fact. I don't think I sold any of the big paintings, but I did sell the whole lot of these small ones. I still meet people who have them. For instance, Douglas Sealy, who bought a picture from my 2002 show at the Taylor Galleries, bought one of those paintings from my very first Dublin exhibition.

You had things like The Billiard Players, *which was based on the Fallon brothers playing in the billiard room of Trevaylor.*

That's right. And there was a painting of our marmalade cat Seán, and one called *Two Lovers on a Bicycle*, which was based on something I'd seen in Dublin.

So you were beginning to paint things you actually saw once again?

Getting closer to it, yes, decidedly.

And then you and Conor adopted your two children in that same year, 1970. You did a number of paintings of them, which were roughly in that style.

Michael Byrne, Nancy
Wynne-Jones, Conor Fallon,
and Seán the cat, Trevaylor,
1965

opposite

Nancy Wynne-Jones
Padraic Fallon
1966, oil on canvas,
102 × 76 cm (40 × 30 in)

Yes, rather Expressionist kind of painting – at least, it started by being Expressionist, with black edges and so on. I used long brushstrokes, and gradually I seemed to want to soften these edges and to blur things together. I found this hard to do technically, because with oil paint you would have to wait for one coat to dry at least a bit before you put a glaze or half-glaze over it. I got very impatient over this and started experimenting with acrylics. The first ones I tried I only worked with a short time. They had just come on to the market and they weren't very good – you know, they had a nasty kind of linoleum finish. So I gave them up and went back to oils, but a few years later I tried them again for the same reason as before, and found that they suited me exactly because they dried pretty quickly. Not so quickly that you couldn't paint wet-into wet if you wanted to, but quickly enough so that you could, in a couple of hours, paint over a totally dry surface. So that development gave me a much bigger range of techniques.

But once again, I began to run out of subject matter, so to speak. There seemed to be a limited number of these kind of subjects that interested me, and I gradually painted less and less. I virtually stopped from about 1970, for almost a year. In saying this, by the way, I'm ignoring the small landscapes in egg tempera, because I was doing those all the time. But those bigger paintings – the Expressionist kind of painting – I effectively ran out of subject matter, and out of ideas for it altogether.

Did you run out of belief in it too?

And my belief in it. So I thought: 'This can't be right, this is absolutely what has happened to me before.' And that discouraged me very much. I thought to myself that since I couldn't do that sort of thing, I would more or less retire into painting still life. This was partly because of our two chil-

NWJ with John and Bridget, her father Charles Wynne-Jones, and his last dog, Kerry, at Penmaenucha, 1970

opposite

Conor Fallon and his father, Padraic Fallon, at Trevaylor, 1971

108

dren, since it proved very difficult to find long stretches of time without interruption, through having to look after them. But it was certainly at that time that I began painting relatively straightforward still lifes.

That went on until your move from Cornwall to Ireland in 1972?

Yes, it did.

Shortly after your marriage, there had been a lot of difficulty over Trevaylor and its occupants, was there not?

Yes, there was a lot of difficulty. It didn't concern the Grahams, though. We bought them a house in Madron, a village a few miles away, which we maintained. They lived there rent-free to the very end of their days. We kept up their allowance for a long time too, until Sydney got some kind of grant or something.

Boots Redgrave had offered to move out of Trevaylor, but when it came to the point she didn't want to. By this stage her husband had virtually left her and was living in London. And she had become involved with a girl called Jacqui who was a much tougher character than Boots, although Boots was good enough at getting her own way. So they took a long time over moving, saying they couldn't find a house and so on, and meanwhile all the artists started taking sides. Eventually we had to buy a house for Boots in Nancledra, and when they were all gone we were finally able to move in. A number of people thought we were treating Boots badly, because her side of the story was very different from the facts. The truth was that she had never paid any rent during the five years she

On the lawn at Trevaylor;
from left: Patricia Fallon,
Valerie Lowndes, Valerie's
niece, Tony O'Malley and
Alan Lowndes, 1965

Alan and Valerie Lowndes
with Alan's nieces, beside
Gurnard's Head, c.1960

Jack Pender and Conor
Fallon sailing in Ted George's
boat, *Father Bob*, in Newlyn
Harbour, 1971

lived in Trevaylor, and had had more than a year to house-hunt. In spite of that, we were depicted as pushing them out at a moment's notice.

And so we were pretty isolated – Peter Lanyon was dead, Bryan Wynter did come over at times, Roger Hilton had become quite impossible. Tony O'Malley had been one of Boots's lodgers and he moved out with her. Somebody who used to come out to us a lot was Alan Lowndes, the North Country painter whom I had known in St Ives before we were married. I first knew him when he was living in a barn in Tremedda, a big farmhouse over near Zennor. He then moved into a house in a village called Halsetown. Alan was a small man with a stammer, who never stopped talking. In spite of that, he was very amusing and highly intelligent, as well as being very well read. He used to call out to Trevaylor with his wife Valerie and their children, and spend the day there. Jack Pender, the Mousehole painter, a very nice man, used to visit us too with his wife and children. Both came a lot at weekends, sometimes together, and that was pleasant, as our children and theirs played together. So we gradually stabilised our situation, but it wasn't ever the same as before.

Alan Lowndes was an excellent painter in a kind of realist mode, using very direct, very strong colour. Some people thought his work was like LS Lowry's, I suppose because they both painted working-class and industrial subjects a lot, but I don't really think so myself. Alan never fitted in with the public school abstractionists who were so strong in Cornwall. He was a truculent little man, who really liked to argue and would keep it up for hours.

And Conor's parents moved over in 1967. His father was in poor health and he took early retirement.

That's right. He wanted to live with Conor, or near him, and so they came over to settle in what was once more called the Little House, where I think they were very happy. They loved the house and they liked being so near to us, and it was wonderful having them just there, seeing them all the time. They were wonderful too with the children. They really were a great comfort to me.

———

Kinsale and Wicklow

Studio Five
1972, acrylic on canvas, 76 × 102 cm (30 × 40 in)

Still Life with Covered Jug
1972, acrylic on canvas, 76 × 63.5 cm (30 × 25 in)

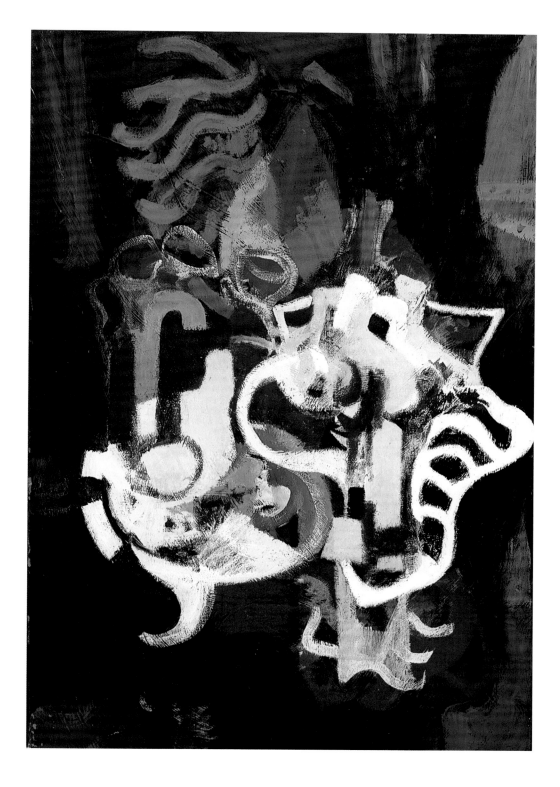

Still Life on Table
1976, acrylic on canvas, 76 × 51 cm (30 × 20 in)

Winter Farm
1980, acrylic on paper, 29 × 41 cm (11.5 × 16.25 in)

The Window
1982, acrylic on paper, 28 × 35 cm (11 × 13.75 in)

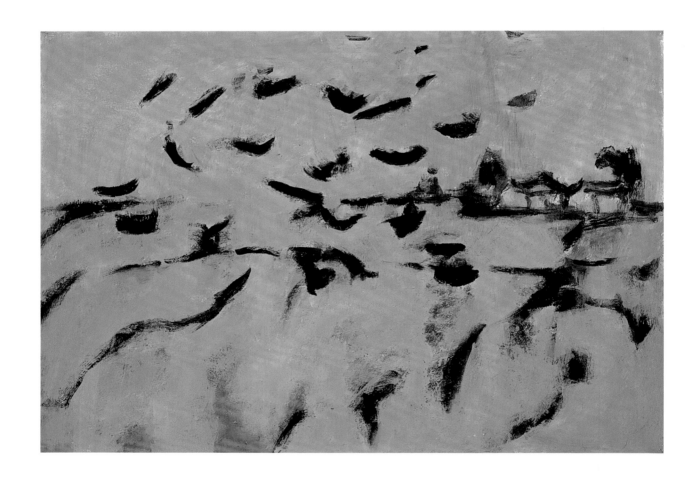

Crows in the Rain
1980, acrylic on paper, 29 x 41 cm (11.5 x 16.25 in)

Farm near Tragumna
1982, acrylic on paper, 29 × 41 cm (11.5 × 16.25 in)

Summer River
1984, acrylic on board, 122 × 152 cm (48 × 60 in)

The Edge of the Tide
1984, acrylic on board, 122 × 152 cm (48 × 60 in), Crawford Municipal Art Gallery, Cork

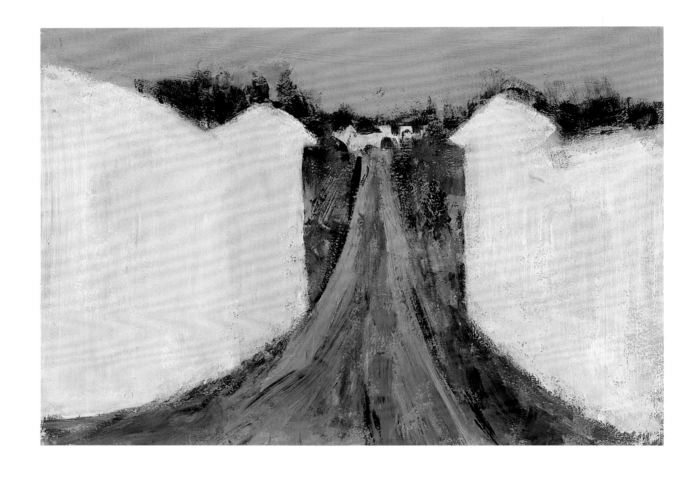

White Gateway
1985, acrylic on paper, 29 × 41 cm (11.5 × 16.25 in), Dúchas, Glebe House and Gallery, Co Donegal

The Buoy
1991, acrylic on paper, 29 x 41 cm (11.5 x 16.25 in)

The Valley
1989, acrylic on paper, 29 × 41 cm (11.5 × 16.25 in)

Red Vineyard
1989, acrylic on paper, 29 × 41 cm (11.5 × 16.25 in), Gerry Watson Collection

Rhododendron Reflected
1990, acrylic on canvas, 127 × 127 cm (50 × 50 in)

Waterlilies
1992, acrylic on canvas, 61 × 76 cm (24 × 30 in)

Pond in October
1990-91, acrylic on canvas, 91.5 × 122 cm (36 × 48 in)

IV

1972–2002: move to Ireland; the challenge of landscape

In 1972 you and Conor took the leap and moved to Ireland. Conor's parents moved back with you.

Yes, mostly because of the children, but in any case the whole St Ives thing had more or less disintegrated by that time. Nearly all the painters we had known – the good ones, that is – had moved out of the area, or moved away altogether, or died, and a lot of young people had moved in, only a few of whom were really serious workers. They were mostly hangers-on who talked about art in the pubs, and a number of them brought down drugs with them, so gradually drugs became a prominent part of the local scene. And we thought this was no place to bring up children. Older people like ourselves could cope with it and ignore it, but it wouldn't be a good environment for growing children. And also, because our children were Irish and had been adopted, we felt they needed as much identity as possible. So we thought we should come back to Ireland.

We had gone there almost every year of those years anyway, and each of us had worked in Ireland for periods. We went over with our caravan and we looked at a whole lot of places where we might live. I'd seen an advertisement – I think in *Country Life* – for this house near Fermoy in Co Cork. It was a beautiful house and we actually bought it, but we were held up for a year by a court case over the custody of our children, and I never lived there.

And then we thought hard about things and felt that we had to be near a city so that there would be good schools available, either in the city or in its neighbourhood. We didn't really want to go back to Dublin, and we thought that Galway was too far away, so that left us Cork. We looked at the various towns by the sea and I think it was Garry, Conor's eldest brother, who suggested Kinsale, because he had been sailing around there and liked it very much. And when we went there and saw it, we though, yes, this is a place that would probably suit us very well. At first we couldn't find any house at all suitable, and we were considering buying a bit of land and building one, but then we heard through the wife of the agent, who was friendly with the owners of Scilly House, that they were thinking of selling. And that's how it came about that we bought it.

That was a house on the edge of Kinsale?

On the edge which they call Scilly, right beside the harbour. It was an 18th-century house that had

Scilly House, Kinsale – the weather-slated house at the top of the picture, with the garden stretching to the water

once been the residence of the Governor of Kinsale. It was a tall house, and we built on studios – one on to what had been a garage, and another just out near the kitchen. I wanted a studio near the kitchen and overlooking the garden so that I could see the children and they could see me in turn, and know I was there.

It was in May 1972 that we moved, and we actually rented a house for six months while the alterations on our own were being completed – the new studios and so on. We wanted my parents-in-law to come too, so we bought a house for them which was practically next to ours; there was just one other house in between. Their place was almost a year being completed, but they moved at the same time as we did.

And you were painting the kind of still life you been doing in Trevaylor?

Yes, I was. They were still lifes painted in rather high colours, and pretty flat. Some were reminis-cences of my nursery as a child, with the checked tablecloth and the milk jug with the muslin top with blue beads around the edge.

Can you describe that particular phase in your development, the first years in Kinsale, I mean?

When we first moved into Scilly House the studios weren't ready, and both of us spent a lot of time in the evening drawing in tiny sketchbooks – little still lifes with ink and coloured inks and sometimes, in my case, in acrylic. Some of them were really nice and I kept my hand in that way, but again I found that I was getting slightly bored with it. Meanwhile I had discovered a book on Persian art by Derek Hill, illustrated just in black and white, but it described how these big temples were covered with tiles – blue and white generally, with white patterns – which completely dissolved the shape of the buildings. I could see this effect even from the photographs.

I was fascinated by it, so eventually I began trying to use the idea on still-life subjects. For instance, I broke up a whole area of the studio – I was in my studio by then – with a number of pots. I'd always liked Eastern-shaped jugs and things like that, and big exotic plants. I had a bit of an Oriental hanging, with elephants and things on it, and this I broke up into all kinds of wavy lines, totally fracturing the space in my studio. The first two paintings I did that way were very successful – they really looked exciting – but I wasn't able to sustain it. However, I painted a lot of them,

and some of them were good; they still look good when I see them today. Others were rather machine-made-looking, and just turned into patterns rather than using the space. But I persevered with them, and in fact I later had two exhibitions of them. Gradually they became less stripy and, I suppose, more Cubist.

Those shows came later in the seventies, at Wally Cole's Emmet Gallery in Dublin, now long gone.

They would have been, yes. They showed that I had been continuing with that technique for quite a long time. I sold a number of them from those exhibitions, which were mounted in 1975 and 1977.

Our son John would have been twelve when we sent him to Bandon Grammar School in 1978, which is fifteen miles from Kinsale. I used to drive him over there every morning, and Conor used to pick him up in the evening. Doing this daily run to Bandon, I became very interested in the landscape round and about, and I started painting it. When I say I 'painting it', I mean I drew these landscapes in a kind of water-based pastel in colour. Then when I came home I could paint in acrylic over the drawings. I continued doing this for a long time.

Jane and Tony O'Malley,
with Nancy Wynne-Jones,
enjoying an autumnal picnic
at Castlehaven, Co Cork,
in 1974

NWJ with Sue Fallon in her
studio, Kinsale, 1974

NWJ and Colman Pearce in
Tony O'Malley's St Ives
house, Seal Cottage, 1981

Manuscript sketch for a composition by Nancy Wynne-Jones, c.1983

You painted a lot of farm gates then, I remember.

Yes, they were the first ones of the *Road to Bandon* series. And then I did some landscapes which were not of the road to Bandon, but they all had gateways in them.

It was the gateway into your future painting.

Kind of interesting. Maybe it was.

Was it at that time that you began to compose music again?

It was about that time, or maybe a little later. That began through Colman Pearce, the conductor. He came down to Kinsale because Conor was a member of a committee for developing the town. They were all trying to think of some way to lengthen the season, and he thought that some kind of music festival might be a good idea. And Charles and Carol Acton, the music critics, introduced us to Colman. So he came down to stay with us. I think it would have been 1977, or perhaps 1978.

One time when he was staying with us, I found a box containing a lot of my student compositions, and I thought it would interest Colman to see them. And to my great surprise, one of them he liked very much and he decided to perform it. He asked me if I still composed and I said I hadn't composed in years. But of course I began thinking about it, and so I began to try and catch up with modern music again. I studied and studied and wrote all the time, until eventually I managed to produce a work which was really quite good and which Colman did perform in Dublin.

This, I think, had a big effect on my work. It was probably through writing the music that I gradually gave up doing still-life paintings altogether, but I continued with the landscapes – the *Road to Bandon* ones, I mean. I hadn't thought they would need a great deal of intellectual content, and the fact that they didn't have made them much freer.

According to Conor, you did a certain number of large or largish pictures around this time, one at least of which related directly to your childhood in Wales. He regards them as essentially intellectual paintings, or concepts. I don't remember seeing any of them myself.

They were intellectual paintings, yes, and probably I had some sort of throwback to my earlier, Herbert Read-influenced ideas. But in retrospect, because of my mother's death around that time, I wanted to record my past in some kind of way, so I did this with a painting called *Walk to the Saltings from Penmaenucha*. I also did one called *Miss Stay and Mrs Gervis*, the two women who gave me lessons in Sherborne, and a painting of Clodgy, a headland off St Ives near the Battery.

I don't think they led to anything much, but basically they were an effort to remember places and their associations. The reason my nostalgia took that particular form was because, years before, an Australian painter in St Ives, Tom Cleghorne, had shown me some photographs of paintings based on walks he'd taken, walks on which he'd seen wild geese and things. I liked them very much. They were rather Lanyonesque, and in fact Lanyon saw them too and liked them. I remembered this as a possible way of dealing with nostalgia.

But you were doing a lot of small paintings in that period, too.

Yes, an enormous number, and I felt genuinely excited by them. I did feel that this finally was the

NWJ with Bridget and John
in Gascony, 1982

right path, that at last I had discovered some relationship with my surroundings and with the landscape I loved. But I found I couldn't do bigger works. I wasn't able to fill in the big areas.

You produced paintings like Badger Road *and a big canvas called* Edge of the Tide, *which impressed me a great deal.*

They were a little later, at the very end of the seventies. I suppose, too, the music I wrote was out of the same energy. For me, that piece performed in Dublin was essentially pictorial – connected with an estuary Conor and I used to visit together, full of sandbanks and wading birds.

After two shows at the Emmet Gallery, you had a joint exhibition with Conor at the Lad Lane Gallery in 1978, showing what you call your 'Cubisty' paintings. Then you moved to the Lincoln Gallery, and your first show there was in 1982. Some of the paintings in that were quite biggish.

Yes, they were a bit bigger, but there were not many paintings on canvas. Paintings of above A2 size I would usually do on canvas, you know, but as I remember these were nearly all on board. But works like the river paintings – *Summer River, Riverrun,* and those – went on to my next exhibition. And they, or some of them anyway, were relatively abstract. You see, I was reluctant to lose that element altogether.

The following exhibitions were at the Hendriks Gallery. Right up to 1988 there, you went on doing relatively large pictures.

Yes. That was no doubt a hangover from my time in St Ives, where it was more or less the law. But with a lot of people, I think, it had come from contact with American big painting. I mean, the paintings were small by American standards, but big by English ones – and of course by Irish standards too.

So you did fairly abstract paintings even still, but they were very firmly based in nature.

They were much more firmly based, yes, and I did feel that I was going in the right direction. The fact that some of the bigger ones were more abstract was because I wasn't able to sustain – or at least I felt that I wasn't able to sustain – a more naturalistic approach on a larger scale, although I attempted to be nearer to what the eye saw.

Can you pinpoint the main reason for that? Was it due to the enlargement of the brushstroke that you used?

Largely the brushstroke, yes, and I was unable to fill large spaces without copying what was before me, in order to fill the spaces. I wasn't able to abstract them in the right way, you know, to find an actual image that emerged out of the painting.

Did you know about the art scene in Ireland when you moved from Cornwall in 1972? You had, of course, visited Ireland a number of times already.

No, I didn't really. I knew about Tony O'Malley, of course, from Cornwall, and I had perhaps heard

Alfresco lunch at Tony and Jane O'Malley's house in Physicianstown, Callan, Co Kilkenny, 1988; from left: Tony O'Malley, Nancy Wynne-Jones, Conor Fallon, Jane and Denis Mitchell

NWJ and Tony O'Malley at the opening of the *Banquet Exhibition* at RHA Gallagher Gallery, Dublin, 1990
(photo: Pat Langan, *Irish Times*)

a few names from Conor. I had my show at the Project in 1970, but I had been unable to go to Dublin to see it because the children had just come to us at that time.

Not long after we moved to Ireland I was introduced to Wally Cole of the Emmet Gallery in Dublin. He ran this gallery largely for emerging artists, and was, is, a lovely, sympathetic man. His stable included people like Charlie Brady and Paddy Graham, so I was in good company. Charlie and his wife Eelagh had stayed with us in Kinsale around 1973. But even in those years, our main contact was with Cornish artists – this was still our world. Robert and Pat Adams, and Denis and Jane Mitchell came to stay with us, and Jack Pender came with his family every year, and of course Tony, who was still the link. But coming to Ireland, although I loved it from the beginning, was in a way a kind of culture shock. I found it a big change from Cornwall, because that part of England was all driven in a particular direction and I thought art in Ireland was very old-fashioned by comparison, when I first came over. I only gradually began to realise the originality of certain artists, such as Paddy Graham, whose work I now admire very much.

You and Conor moved from Kinsale to Co Wicklow in 1988. Can you describe the reason, or reasons, for this move?

The period in Kinsale was important for both of us because we were relatively isolated down there. There were no other artists we knew within easy reach. Occasionally one might come and stay with us, but only as a visitor. That meant we could work quite privately, and experiment without feeling self-conscious about it. And so it was a very important time. But by then we both had a gallery in Dublin, and it was awkward bringing work up and down. We also began to feel the need to talk to other artists and to take more part in an artist's life.

Our children at the time were going to college, up to Trinity, and Conor's parents had died, so it seemed the perfect time to move. We felt that when we were up there we would be nearer to at least some of the family – you know, to you and your brother Niall, and it would be no farther away from Garry in Wexford. So we made the move in the end.

Can you describe the influence, if any, of Wicklow on your painting? It was a big change from a small southern seaport to a rural spot in east Leinster. And by that stage, surely, you had used up your Road to Bandon?

I'd used it up by then, yes. I felt that although I had been excited by it at the time – and in fact I continued to like it – all the same it wasn't actually my country. I had rather to force myself to find subjects in it, hence the number of gateposts, for instance! When I came to Wicklow, of course, I was excited by the mountains. After all I am from Wales, and a mountainous part of Wales too. But I found the trees a difficulty, because I'd never been accustomed to painting trees and I wasn't terribly interested in doing so either. When we moved into Ballard House, near Rathdrum, Conor built a gallery at one end of my studio with a big window which looked over the mountain, Ballinacor. And I painted a large number of pictures of that.

When we first came there I painted the pond a lot too. That was a very fecund source for me, our pond – the beautiful colour of the water, and the little island in the middle with all kinds of exotic plants gathered around the edge. It could look quite tropical at times, which was very stimulating.

For several years, that pond became one of your leitmotiven, like Seán McSweeney with his bit of Sligo bog. Did you paint it all the year round?

I painted it mostly in the autumn because I particularly like those autumnal colours, especially in the trees growing about the pond. One of the reasons why I like going to Mayo so much is that the bogs there, at a certain time of year, go that orange tone. Conor is planning to set up little tables and benches by our pond so that I can sit around and draw it from all angles. I might try doing paintings then directly from the motif, rather than drawing it and working it up later in the studio. With a lot of foliage and vegetation, it can be difficult to draw them properly.

I like painting water. I have done a good many paintings with water in them over the years. I don't actually paint the lakes or ponds in Mayo much, admittedly, because I like this flat space of the bogs stretching in front of me. There is a special kind of challenge in how to convey the sense that there is a stark watery depth underneath all that surface brightness. Yet I did not paint the sea much in Cornwall. I don't know why exactly. A wave is a very beautiful thing, but I haven't been able to make anything out of it. I suppose it's something which is complete in itself. And then we all know Courbet's great paintings of waves, and you can't do much with the subject after those. Besides, I need a background to what I paint, like mountains in a landscape, while the sea just goes on and on.

The pond at Ballard House

You and Conor visited France a number of times in the late eighties and early nineties, and you did a lot of painting there in those years.

My first exhibition at the Taylor Galleries in 1990 was almost entirely of French paintings on a small scale, and I didn't have any big abstract pieces in that show. They were all small works on paper. I thought this was right at that time, this was how I should paint. But I would also have liked to paint slightly larger pictures which were less about the surface, and more about the image of the place.

Seamus Heaney, in a note to me, said that the paintings in my most recent [2002] exhibition were, as he put it, 'place and palette and spirit, all equal', and I think that is exactly what I would like them to be.

And is that precisely what you feel you are doing now?

I do. I feel all the time that I can improve on this, that I can go in deeper, produce paintings that are more exciting in colour and technique, but basically that's right. I'm painting as well as I can at the moment, yes.

In this most recent exhibition you have shown that you're able to do that equally well on a larger scale. John Taylor was saying that it was the first show in which there wasn't a difference between your big canvases and your small works on paper.

That's true, I think. I really feel that, for the first time, I'm painting to my full potential.

How do you see your painting in relation to the past, to its development?

If you leave out the branches which ended off, the main line has gone on right the way through. I see my paintings of the fifties and sixties are very like what I do now. The thing is now I'm more confident, and so I can do this more regularly. I think they are richer in handling also; again this is a matter of confidence, of being able to put down what you want and leave it, and just go over the top of it if you want to. You don't ever get rid of it.

And I have found various ways of treating space which I hadn't at that time. I was concerned with keeping the integrity of the picture surface, which was something of our time. I painted the small paintings in the landscape with an ordinary academic kind of space, and gradually I began to be able to float paint marks over this. This created a kind of space in between the eye and the distance in this landscape, because when you look over a big landscape you see the horizon line – which is why it is very important to have it – but in between you see all kinds of things which move in and out of focus as you move your eye around. So in a way you can put almost anything anywhere and it will be all right, providing it is something you have seen there. You have to translate this again so they become paint marks which are evocative to somebody else as well as yourself. They fill in the space and make the painting surface as interesting as looking at the real landscape. It is an equivalent for it.

And what about translating things from a large scale to a small scale?

That's important, because when you are looking out on a landscape it's huge and comes all around

NWJ with Pat Taylor
(he and his brother John
have been her dealers for
many years) and his wife
Martina, 1991

Co Mayo
(photo: Barry Segrave)

NWJ drawing at the Gap
of the Wind, Co Mayo,
2001

you, and you're trying to put this onto a little bit of paper perhaps 12 inches by 18, so you have to select, you have to abstract what you're going to put there. Otherwise it is going to be a total muddle. You've picked this landscape because it seems to you significant, so you have to decide what actual features are of significance to you and you have to translate them into this tiny little object you have in front of you so they seem equally significant, give back the same vibrations.

Do you feel there is a particular development or direction that your work is going at the moment?

No. I just follow the painting rather than the painting following me. I hope to continue to go up to Mayo where I like to paint the big bogs. That's my favourite thing to paint.

You painted originally in Mayo on some kind of American fellowship. Can you describe that experience?

In 1994 we were given this fellowship by the Ballinglen Foundation, set up by an American couple, the Maxwells. It gave us a cottage to work in for anything up to two months – and actually we went for six weeks – over in Ballycastle on the north coast of Mayo. I was instantly entranced by the huge space over the big bogs and around the coast, and the coastline itself – its huge black cliffs, and moorlands which went right down to the edge. Along the coast the colour isn't always interesting, but the sweep and turn of the land is very interesting. But I finally homed in on these big bogs which are generally great stretches of more or less flat land with mountains on the edge. There seems to me to be endless space, and that's what I love about it, and the ancient and primeval feeling to the space too.

It's probably similar to where I was born in Wales, although it is much more mountainous where I was born; I mean the mountains are much closer. Where my home was in Wales I looked across a tidal river valley with rushes and things, across to a heather-covered mountain on the other side. So I had this feeling of wide space before you suddenly came up against something and went upright instead of horizontal. That appeals to me.

And Nephin, that's a sacred mountain. That I love. It is a wonderful shape and – it's a curious thing – it appears almost everywhere you go in Mayo. You think you've left Nephin behind, but

The garden at Enniscoe, Co Mayo. The second dormer from the left is the bedroom window from which there is a view of Nephin

View of Nephin from the bedroom window in Enniscoe, Co Mayo (see *Good Morning Nephin* and *Nephin at Sunrise*)

suddenly there it is in front of you; you can't see how it could possible have arrived there. I also see it from my bedroom window at the cottage we have in Enniscoe.

It was because, as I say, I was so excited by this space that I felt I had to express it in some kind of way. When you look out at it, when you're just looking at a wide landscape, it seems full of incident, but if you put it down on paper there is a huge blankness and a kind of empty feeling, and all this space. When you are there the very air seems full of colour, because you take down colour from the sky and from down below – the green of the grass, for instance. As your eye moves about, you shift the colour with it, with the flick of your eye, to and fro.

You get after-images too, and things you see out of the corner of your eye. When you're painting one corner of a landscape, the rest of it is coloured by the fact that what you're painting down in this left-hand corner might be a whole lot of buttercups, and what you see out of the rest of your eyes is coloured because of this. And so I began to fill in the space with kind of misty shapes in order to keep the impression that what you saw, really saw, was a bit more than what you intellectually understood. I mean, I became more and more interested in what the eye actually sees, as apart from what it thinks it sees.

Depicting the air and atmosphere is important in your work. Could you say a little more about that.

The air around one is actually filled with excitement. When you look at it it seems its transparent, but it also has almost subliminal colours, which you have picked up from all over the place. Your eye moves round and picks up this and that, some things in focus and some things out of focus. Bonnard was marvellous at this. When you are outside looking at the landscape you have the atmosphere around you and all over you, and somehow you have to give the impression that this is the case. I often, in fact, pull the sky into the painting in some way

Texture is important to you too.

Again, it is a feature of any landscape. It is a feature of these bogs that I paint. When you look down around your feet, the bogs are mossy and they are grassy and there are holes in them where the spade has been in, and all this texture is tremendously interesting. But you can't paint it exactly as it is. In the first place you can't, and if you did, it wouldn't look good – it would look like an old photograph or something – so you have to discover, usually in the course of doing it, some way of making your actual paint marks convey the same interesting complexity. You won't, perhaps, make them in the least the same, but they will be an equivalent for them, which will give you the same kind of sensation of richness that the land does.

Are you a disciplined painter. Do you have a routine of painting?

I am, in as much as I paint every day. I don't exactly make a point of it. Its just naturally the thing that I do. If I didn't do it I'd be bored. I may paint for a couple of hours, or I might only paint for half an hour. But if I'm painting for half an hour its because I've just come out and found there's just a little bit to do. Nowadays I don't paint in the afternoons, although I used to. But I never painted tremendously long hours and I don't know any good painter who does. I think that it is very intense when you are painting. If Conor comes in when I'm painting I jump five feet high if I haven't see him coming.

How do you start the process of making a painting?

Nancy Wynne-Jones and
Conor Fallon at Ballard
House, Co Wicklow, 1992
(photo: Pat Langan, *Irish Times*)

NWJ in her studio at
Ballard House, 1992
(photo: Pat Langan, *Irish Times*)

I go out into the landscape. I go out in the car and I see something that interests me and I do an oil pastel drawing in colour. Occasionally I do one in black and white, but not very often now, nearly always in colour, and as I draw I decide what's interesting about the landscape. I go into my studio and look through my drawings, and then have to decide which one I will paint. I have to decide what scale it would have most significance in. Having decided that I then sometimes draw in the main features in paint, perhaps blue. Sometimes I do them straight away in the colour they are going to be, but probably a little lighter than they will be eventually because that gives more glow to the painting. And then I just work away. I work over the whole area of the painting. I don't ever complete one bit and then go on to the next, insofar as one can do that. I work over the whole thing. I finish it at a certain point, up to a degree, when I think that's all I can do at the moment, that's somewhere fairly near it.

Now I've got to sit back and have a look at it and see how I can go on, and then I go again and paint a bit more. I see something that I know is wrong. And having done that it alters everything else. So I do this time and time again, and work over the whole thing all the time. I don't correct, exactly; I just paint on top so it becomes almost a palimpsest in the end too, which gives a kind of richness – until the time comes when I think that's it, I don't think I can do any more, that's as near as I can get to what I want to say.

I suppose the time it takes it varies enormously.

Yes. Generally a 30 x 40 inch canvas would take me perhaps a month, working most days, but I only ever do one painting at a time. A lot of people do several paintings at a time, but I get very focused on the one thing.

Do you have a vision of what a painting is going to be like before you begin?

A very vague one, yes.

I remember your saying you like to see the history of a painting being made in the painting.

I think that is a kind of honesty in painting. You don't want to paint out everything that was wrong the first time – although you will do so as you go along – but you don't want to deliberately destroy your first thoughts about the subject, because that way you get a feeling of time as well, the time that it took you to paint it. So the painting becomes a picture of time as well as subject.

And, of course, the struggle as well.

It's a struggle, but one hopes that doesn't come out too much. I like it to look in the end as though it was quite casually put down, because the paint stroke is more interesting then – it has life in it. You don't want a dead, careful thing.

And do you now find your painting intellectually satisfying, as you always wanted it to be?

I do. But perhaps because of that I have to think up ways of dealing with it which are organic ways, not intellectually imposed on my work.

With what Irish artists do you feel an affinity now?

I have a great admiration for Patrick Collins. I think his work is tremendously original at its best. I didn't really appreciate the greatness of Jack Yeats until I lived in Ireland and came to know the west. I like Barrie Cooke, especially his early paintings based on water and fish, and Camille Souter, and of course Tony O'Malley, and perhaps most of all Seán McSweeney, whose approach to landscape I feel very much in sympathy with. I also think Basil Blackshaw is a superb painter.

We became close friends of Alexandra Wejchert, and I greatly admired the abstract rigour of her sculpture. Melanie le Brocquy is a good friend too, and I think her work has great warmth. I also like the honesty of Imogen Stuart's sculpture. Imogen is also a friend of ours. Breon O'Casey comes to stay with us in Wicklow most years. One year we were in Mayo together. I enjoyed immensely having him work in the Ballinglen studio next to mine, and I think he enjoyed it too. And I also admire very much the work of the American sculptor Bill Freeland, who lives part of the year in Mayo with his painter-wife Magda. They are close friends of ours.

You are an honorary RHA and a member of Aosdána. Do those organisations have significance for you?

I have shown at the RHA for a number of years – firstly, because Conor was the secretary there, and in any case, as time went by, it was a place where an increasingly large spectrum of Irish art was on the wall and I felt I would like to be part of it. The Honorary Council dinner is tremendous fun.

I think of Aosdána as a gathering of all the best artists in Ireland. I was very pleased to be considered one of them, when I was elected.

There seems to be a general agreement, or at least an assumption, that we are now in the phase of art history known as Post-Modernism. What does the term mean to you, if it means anything?

For myself, it seems a defeatist kind of thing, using your experience of the art of the past to produce a kind of pastiche. It does that not for really creative reasons, but in a spirit which implies that none of this is important, that it's all a kind of intellectual game. The further implication is that it has no real meaning because there is no meaning in life. And it goes along with the total lack of any belief in the spiritual nowadays; by 'spiritual', by the way, I don't mean religion. I think there is no point in art if it has no spiritual significance. After all, why do it if there is none? I know Francis

Breon and Doreen O'Casey with Nancy Wynne-Jones at Ballard House, Co Wicklow, 1995

Bacon often said that there was no meaning in things, that art for him was all a sort of play, but his painting itself is not at all like that. In fact, he was almost fanatically involved in what he did.

I think also that an awful lot of the art I see around is curiously Victorian, in the sense that it is essentially illustrative – that is, illustrative of an idea or 'conceit', not of an incident or anecdote, as in the past. These people take some conceit – sometimes very slight or trivial in itself – and illustrate it, and the whole thing then becomes terribly one-dimensional. Somehow, it seems that so many young artists have lost all belief in the visual, even though what they do is still supposed to be visual art. I would have thought there was enough of interest in the world we see and experience to keep one going for ever.

If you want intellectual content, then you should consider that every object we see is made up of millions of atoms in motion. We all know now that nothing is in fact solid, nothing is permanent, and all our awareness of that adds to the mystery of what we see, rather than decreasing it. We know, for instance, that nothing really has a colour, that this depends on the light and various other factors, and also that it depends on whom or what sees it, and from where. A cat sees everything in grey, I understand. So with all that to deal with I cannot see any necessity for getting involved in these little conceits or pseudo-intellectual problems.

When I look at lists of galleries and exhibitions, in London and in other places, I cannot think of a single one about which I could say, 'Oh, I'd love to see that'. Of course, this may be, at least partly, a question of loss of contact between different generations – the generation gap as it's called. There comes a time when an artist doesn't understand the artists coming after him or her. But then, quite probably, the good ones among them are still known to relatively few people. Very often that is the case, in fact. Probably there are good painters working away in relative obscurity, about whom we hear nothing, for the moment anyway.

One chapter in your painting we haven't mentioned is your visit to South Africa. You spent a month there in 1998 and produced a body of work from that. Can you describe the impact it made on you?

South Africa was just fantastic. It was infinitely the most beautiful place I have ever been in my life. Everything about it was marvellous – the scale of it, and the beauty of it. It felt incredibly ancient, so ancient that all human life was just a blip in its long history. So mysterious.

I think the colour of South Africa had a big effect on my work. The light there was extraordinary – a kind of creamy light – and the shadows were purple, not blue. The earth being red made me feel that this was the basic colour of Africa. I often painted landscapes with a red sky, which gave that primeval character. Oddly enough, the landscape in Mayo has something of the same quality. And it intensified the feeling I have about landscape anyway – that we are set down in this extraordinary world and have to find our place in it, which I and other artists try to do through our work.

BRIAN FALLON was born in Cootehill, Co Cavan, in 1933, and was educated at Trinity College Dublin. He was art critic with the Irish Times for 35 years, and was also literary editor from 1977 to 1988. He is the author of *Irish Art 1830-1990*, and *An Age of Innocence*, a history of Irish culture from 1930 to 1960, as well as various monographs. He has edited the collected poems of his father, the poet Padraic Fallon, for Carcanet Press.

BARBARA ANN TAYLOR was born and brought up near Dublin, and educated at Trinity College Dublin and Oxford University. She has worked in various museums and galleries, including the National Gallery of Ireland and the Victoria & Albert Museum, London. She was art critic for several years with *Harpers & Queen*.

Mayo

Humbert's Landing
1994, acrylic on paper, 42 × 58.5 cm (16.5 × 23 in)

Ballinglen
1994, acrylic on paper, 42 × 58.5 cm (16.5 × 23 in)

Cregennan Lake
1997-98, acrylic on canvas, 122 × 152 cm (48 × 60 in)

Mountain and Cornfield
1996, acrylic on canvas, 76 × 102 cm (30 × 40 in)

Pond with Orange Tree and Little House
1997, acrylic on canvas, 76 × 102 cm (30 × 40 in)

The Islands
1996, acrylic on canvas, 152 × 122 cm (60 × 48 in)

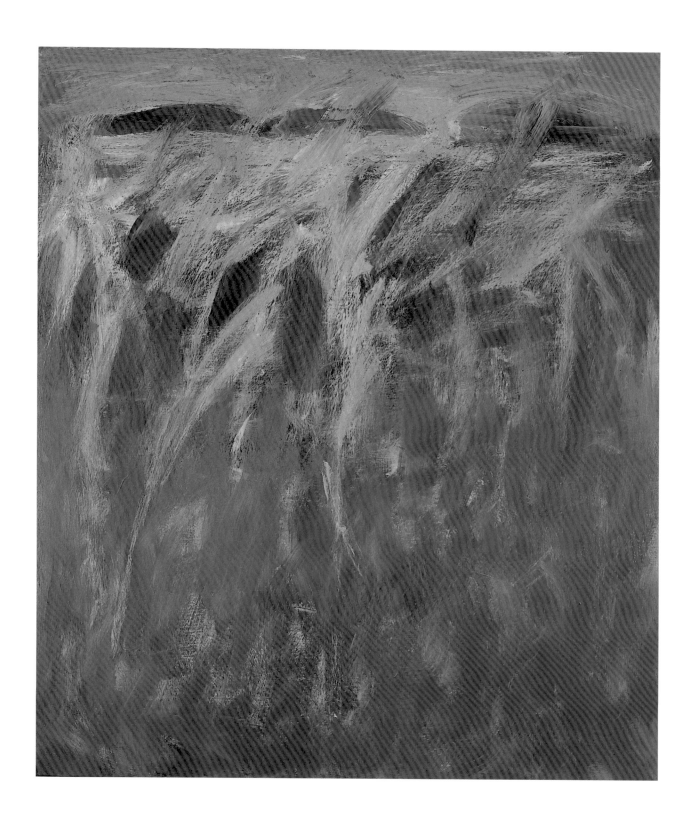

Bushman's Kloof, Evening
1998, acrylic on paper, 42 × 58.5 cm (16.5 × 23 in)

Cape of Good Hope
1998, acrylic on canvas, 76 × 102 cm (30 × 40 in)

Klein Constantia
1998, acrylic on paper, 42 × 58.5 cm (16.5 × 23 in)

The Little Mosque
1998, acrylic on paper, 42 × 58.5 cm (16.5 × 23 in)

High Bog
2000, acrylic on paper, 42 × 58.5 cm (16.5 × 23 in)

Yellow Bog
1999, acrylic on canvas, 102 × 76 cm (40 × 30 in)

Pale Bog
2000, acrylic on paper, 42 × 58.5 cm (16.5 × 23 in)

Across to Achill
2000, acrylic on paper, 42 × 58.5 cm (16.5 × 23 in)

Nephin in the Evening
2001, acrylic on paper, 29 × 41 cm (11.5 × 16.25 in)

Green Summer Bog
2001, acrylic on paper, 42 x 58.5 cm (16.5 x 23 in)

Pale Bog
2001, acrylic on canvas, 76 × 102 cm (30 × 40 in)

Corvoley
2001, acrylic on canvas, 76 × 102 cm (30 × 40 in)

Dark Moor with Nephin
2001, acrylic on canvas, 76 × 102 cm (30 × 40 in)

Summer Bog with Pink Grass and Meadowsweet
2001, acrylic on paper, 42 × 58.5 cm (16.5 × 23 in)

Dark Bog with Meadowsweet
2001, acrylic on paper, 42 x 58.5 cm (16.5 x 23 in)

Bog with White Farms
2001, acrylic on paper, 42 × 58.5 cm (16.5 × 23 in)

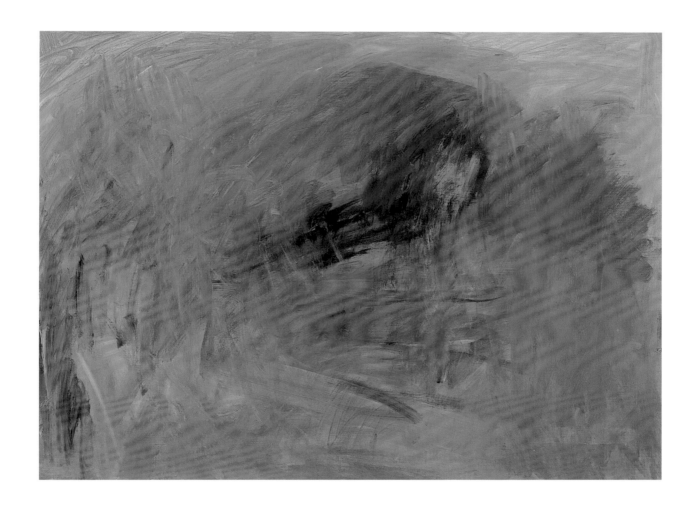

Good Morning Nephin
2001, acrylic on canvas, 76 × 102 cm (30 × 40 in)

Errew Bog with Nephin
2001, acrylic on paper, 29 × 41 cm (11.5 × 16.25 in)

Nephin at Sunrise
2001, acrylic on paper, 29 × 41 cm (11.5 × 16.25 in)

ARTISTS AND PERSONALITIES MENTIONED

ADAMS, Robert (1917-1984) – English sculptor with an international reputation, particularly for his pieces in welded steel. Born in Northampton, he first studied art there. He carried out many important commissions (including Gelsenkirchen State Theatre, Essen, and New Custom House, Heathrow Airport), but was also noted for his superb small bronzes with their fastidious finish. Adams was not part of the St Ives School, but he had friends and admirers there. He taught for a time in nearby Falmouth, and bore rather the same relation to St Ives painterly abstraction as, in America, the sculptor David Smith did to the Abstract Expressionists.

ALWYN, William (1905-1985) – English composer, born in Northampton. He attended the Royal Academy of Music where eventually became Professor of Composition. Also played in the London Symphony Orchestra as a flautist. His many film scores – one was for Carol Reid's *Odd Man Out* – tended to overshadow his 'serious' compositions, which included five symphonies, two operas, song cycles and instrumental music.

BENJAMIN, Anthony (1931-2002) – English painter, sculptor, printmaker and engraver on glass, born in Hampshire. He began as an engineering student but later studied painting under Léger in Paris. A man of marked independence, he served a prison term as a conscientious objector, and once fought as a professional boxer to fund his art studies. Benjamin settled in Cornwall in the early 1950s. Won awards to study in France (under Stanley Hayter) and in Italy. Later in his career he taught in Canada and the US. An exhibition, *Works on Paper*, was mounted by Gimpel Fils in London in 1990.

BLACKSHAW, Basil (1932-) – Northern Irish painter, one of whose works was acquired by the Ulster Museum when he was only 21. Born in Glengormley, Co Antrim, and precociously gifted, he studied at the Belfast College of Art. With a rural background and interests, he was often drawn to painting horses and dogs, but his treatment of these grew increasingly broad and emblematic, close at times to 'New Image' painting. Has also painted many nudes, landscapes and flower pieces, as well as some striking portraits. Member of Aosdána and an HRHA. Now lives and paints in Antrim, within sight of Lough Neagh.

BRADY, Charles (1926-1997) – American painter of partly Irish descent. Born in New York, where he studied at the Art Students' League and met Franz Kline and de Kooning. Came to Ireland first in the 1950s. In the 1960s he settled in Dun Laoghaire, marrying the actress Eelagh Noonan, and helped to found the Independent Artists, though Brady was essentially a maverick figure. Exhibited many times in Dublin, but was also included in prestige shows in America. In an era largely dominat-ed by abstract art, he preferred to paint still life and landscape with a rather muted palette. A retrospective was mounted at the RHA Gallagher Gallery in 2002. Member of Aosdána and an HRHA.

BYRNE, Michael (1921-1989) – Irish painter and printmaker. Born in Dublin, he worked originally as a dental mechanic but attended lessons at the National College of Art & Design, Dublin. Visited Spain in 1952, and also made many trips to France. His early works were in a realist-expressionist vein, but later he moved into abstraction, producing particularly sensitive and elegant screenprints. Active in founding the Independent Artists in 1960 and in setting up the Project Gallery (later Project Arts Centre). Also a founder member of the Black Church Print Studio and an original Aosdána member. Part-time teacher at NCAD from 1971 to 1979.

CANNEY, Michael (1923-2001) – English painter and graphic artist, born in Falmouth. Also curator, writer, lecturer and broadcaster. He studied at the Penzance School of Art, and later at Goldsmiths' College in London. During war service in Italy he met de Chirico. Canney, like many of his generation, was influenced by Ben Nicholson, but retained his own quietly individual style. For a number of years he was director of Newlyn Art Gallery, where he mounted a number of seminal exhibitions. As an independent personality, Canney was much liked and respected in Cornish art circles.

CLOUGH, Prunella (1919-1999) – English painter and printmaker, associated at first with the circle of Colquhoun, MacBryde and Minton, but moving eventually into abstraction or semi-abstraction. Born in London, she studied at the Chelsea School of Art and later became a part-time teacher there. At first she painted mainly fishermen, lorry-drivers, industrial buildings and sites, often with a rather sombre palette. Later, probably influenced by the new American painting, she developed an abstract vocabulary, though hints of her former subject matter remained. Clough was a niece of the pioneer designer Eileen Gray.

COLLINS, Patrick (1910-1994) – Irish painter, one of the most gifted to emerge from under the shadow of Jack Yeats. Born in Co Sligo, he worked in a Dublin insurance office and was middle-aged before he painted full-time. Collins' mature style is misty, often blue-grey in tone, but with emerging motifs which are sharply defined – a bog cutting, a small farm. A man of striking looks, he was a prominent figure in Dublin bohemia. Collins was given a retrospective exhibition at Trinity College Dublin in 1981, but the real upsurge in his reputation has come since his death. Member of Aosdána and an HRHA.

COOKE, Barrie (1931-) – painter, born in Cheshire, he studied art history at Harvard and attended various summer schools of painting in the US and Europe. Came to Ireland in the 1950s, and for years lived in Co Kilkenny, but has since moved to Co Sligo. His style is lyrical, colourful and fluent, with some debt to Abstract Expressionism and hints of *Tachisme*. Cooke is particularly fascinated by water (he is a keen fisherman), and many of his finest paintings are of lakes, rivers and freshwater fish. He is a member of Aosdána. Large-scale exhibition at The Hague in 1992.

DEMUTH, Norman (1898-1968) – English musician, born in Croydon, died in Chichester. Studied at the Royal College of Music in London and later taught at the Royal Academy of Music. A prolific composer, he produced four symphonies and five concertos, five operas (including one on Ben Jonson's play *Volpone*), five ballets and a quantity of instrumental music. As well as composing and teaching, Demuth also wrote books on Ravel, Roussel, Dukas, Franck and Gounod.

FALLON, Conor (1939-) – Irish sculptor, born in Dublin, and the third son of the poet Padraic Fallon (1905-1974). He began as a painter but – partly on the advice of Denis Mitchell – turned to sculpture. Married Nancy Wynne-Jones in 1966 and lived in Cornwall. They returned to Ireland in 1972 and settled in Kinsale. Has had numerous one-man exhibitions, both in public and private galleries, figured in group shows of Irish art abroad, and has carried out some major commissions. Now lives in a rural area of Co Wicklow. A member of Aosdána and an RHA.

FALLON, Padraic (1905-1974) – Irish poet, born in Athenry, Co Galway. As a young civil servant in Dublin, he came under the influence of AE (George Russell), published his first poem when he was 18, and by his forties was ranked with MacNiece, Clarke and Kavanagh. He turned his attention to verse plays for radio in the 1950s, performed on Radio Éireann, the BBC, and in many European countries. It was not until 1974, the year of his death, that Dolmen Press published a collection. *Poems and Versions* (Carcanet Press) followed in 1983, and *Collected Poems* in 1990 (Carcanet / Gallery Press). Carcanet will publish *Selected Poems* in 2003 and three verse plays in 2005 to mark the centenary of his birth.

FEATHERSTONE, Bill (1928-) – Canadian-born sculptor, also a painter, who lived and worked in the St Ives area for eleven years, eventually returning to Canada. Much of his sculpture was in wood, but during the 1960s he also experimented with Op and Kinetic art. He later became an art teacher in his native country, while having a number of exhibitions there. His genial, extrovert temperament made him a popular figure in Cornwall.

FREELAND, Bill (1929-) – American sculptor who, since 1992, has strongly identified himself with the west of Ireland, spending part of every year in Mayo. Born in

Pittsburgh but with Virginian blood, he trained at first as a painter, studying under Hans Hofmann. Lived and worked for a time in New York, but generally prefers a rural ambience; the farming implements of his youth are a lasting memory. Cubist-style collage and other influences gradually led him into sculpture, with emphasis on assemblage-like works which sometimes incorporate found objects. Married to the painter Magda Vitale.

FROST, Terry (now Sir Terry, 1915-) – English painter and printmaker, born in Leamington Spa, and a prominent figure in St Ives and English art from the 1950s onwards. During WW II he spent time in a prisoner-of-war camp, where he managed to draw and paint. First moved to St Ives in 1946 to study there, returning in 1957 to paint full-time but later moving to Newlyn. Frost had personal contacts with the American Abstract Expressionists, and showed in New York. He is known as an inspiring teacher. Retrospective at the London Tate in 2001.

GABO, Naum (1890-1977) – Russian sculptor, younger brother of Antoine Pevsner. The great Constructivist sculptor lived and worked at Carbis Bay, near St Ives, from 1939 to 1946, when he left for the US. He had emigrated from Russia in 1922, settling in Berlin and later in Paris. In 1935 he moved to London. Gabo had a major influence on painters such as Lanyon and John Wells, as well as on fellow sculptors. During his final years of world fame in America, where he took US citizenship, Gabo retained a genuine feeling for Britain, and he left the Tate Gallery a collection of small works and maquettes. In return, he was given a knighthood in 1971.

GRAHAM, WS (1918-1986) – Scottish poet from Greenock, usually called Sydney, who became an integral part of the Cornish art scene. He was associated with the Neo-Romanticism of the 1940s, when he was friendly with Dylan Thomas, but his poetic voice is more colloquial and realist. Graham was a friend of many painters, and addressed poems to Lanyon, O'Malley and Hilton, among others. In Cornwall he worked for a time as a part-time coastguard and also on local fishing-boats – an experience embodied in his best-known work, *The Night Fishing* (1955). Graham's *Collected Poems* was published by Faber & Faber in 1979. His wife Nessie Dunsmuir (1909-1999) was also a poet.

GRAHAM, Patrick (1943-) – Irish painter, born in Mullingar, Co Westmeath. Precociously gifted, he was a student at National College of Art & Design in Dublin in his teens. A spell in advertising threatened to disrupt his career, and it was not until the 1970s that Graham seemed to rediscover his self-belief as a painter. His quasi-Expressionist style is individual and idiosyncratic, embracing sex, religion, humour, political issues and visceral self-analysis. As well as having numerous one-man shows in Dublin, he exhibits with the Jack Rutberg

Gallery in Los Angeles. Å member of Aosdána, Graham is represented in numerous public collections.

HAYMAN, Patrick (1915-1988) – London-born painter and graphic artist, he spent much of his early life in New Zealand. He lived in Mevagissey, Cornwall, in 1950, and in St Ives from 1951 to 1953, then moved to London but returned to St Ives for a year in 1964-65. Something of a maverick in the Cornish art world because of his individual and quirkily figurative style, which was charged with imagination and wit. Hayman was also a poet who illustrated his own poems, achieving a Blakean unity of text and image, and he founded and edited the influential magazine *The Painter and Sculptor*. From 1960 he lived in Barnes, but still paid regular visits to Cornwall.

HEATH, John Rippiner (1887-1950) – Birmingham-born medical doctor, composer, conductor and inspirational personality. Heath showed conspicuous musical talent while at school in Bristol and later at Cambridge University, but he opted for medicine as a career, setting up as a GP in Barmouth, Merionethshire. During WW I he served in Salonika, resuming his practice in 1919 while composing prolifically. Heath became recognised as one of Britain's leading young musicians, but after 1925 his stock apparently declined, though he remained active in Welsh musical life. He practiced in Barmouth until his death, but many of his manuscripts were lost.

HEPWORTH, Dame Barbara (1903-1975) – Leeds-born sculptor with an international reputation, noted as much for her powerful, articulate personality as for her works in wood, stone, marble and bronze. She moved to St Ives in 1939 with her then husband Ben Nicholson, with whom she formed a formidable partnership that lasted into the late 1950s. Hepworth won many awards and honours, and her sculptures stand in many public sites as well as in public and private collections. Her studio in St Ives is now a museum in her memory. Denis Mitchell and Breon O'Casey both worked for a time as her assistants.

HERON, Patrick (1920-1999) – born in Headingly, Leeds, he grew up mainly in Cornwall. He studied at the Slade (1937-39), and after the war became a prominent critic and lecturer, as well as a painter and printmaker. At first Heron's style was strongly oriented towards Paris, but later he came under the influence of American abstraction, which he was one of the first English critics to acclaim. Showed at the Venice Biennale in 1964. His book *The Changing Forms of Art* had a wide influence, as did his challenging art criticism. Heron was awarded a CBE in 1977, and was given a retrospective exhibition at the Tate Gallery in London shortly before his death.

HILTON, Roger (1911-1975) – born in Northwood, Middlesex, of German-Jewish descent, he was a prominent painter of the St Ives School. He studied at the Slade and in Paris under Roger Bissière. During WW II he was taken prisoner and held until 1945. Hilton's abstract style won him wide acclaim, including a prize at the Venice Biennale in 1964, but his last years were shadowed by illness and alcoholism – though the figurative gouaches he produced marked a new departure. In 1980 his widow, Rose Hilton (herself a talented painter), published his *Night Letters and Selected Drawings*, a classic of its kind. His first wife, Ruth Hilton (1921-1995), to whom he was married from 1947 to 1963, was a professional musician and teacher.

IRVIN, Albert (1922-) – painter and printmaker, born in London, and studied at Northampton School of Art. Saw service as a rear-gunner in the RAF (1941-46). In the postwar years he studied at Goldsmiths' College of Art in London, where he later taught for many years (1962-83). Won major British Arts Council awards in 1968 and 1975. Irvin began as a figurative artist, but later developed a broad, colourful abstract style, freely and almost splashily painted, and on an increasingly large scale. Has won international success in recent years.

LANYON, Peter (1918-1964) – British postwar artist, achieving an international reputation before he had reached 40, but dying tragically after a gliding accident when he was at the height of his powers. Born in St Ives, Lanyon studied in Penzance and at the Euston Road School of Art. During WW II he served as an air force technician. He was one of the few native-born Cornishmen among the St Ives group, generally basing his style in landscape, but developing it into a powerful and original version of Abstract Expressionism. Lanyon was also influential and inspiring as a teacher and lecturer in St Ives, Falmouth and Corsham. The scale and vitality of his mature paintings (e.g. *St Just* (1953)) dwarf those of most of his contemporaries.

LEACH, Bernard (1887-1979) – English potter, also a writer on art and an aesthetic philosopher. He was born in Hong Kong and studied painting and etching in London, but turned increasingly to pottery, which he helped to elevate to a higher status. Leach spent many years in the Far East, where he was influenced by Korean folk ceramics in particular. In partnership with the Japanese potter Shoji Hamada, he set up the Leach Pottery near St Ives, where he gradually took on the status of a guru. In his long, productive and influential life, Leach did much to abolish the barrier between 'art' and 'craft'. His second wife, the American-born Janet Leach, was also a gifted potter.

LE BROCQUY, Melanie (1919-) – Irish sculptor, sister of the painter Louis le Brocquy. Born in Dublin, she studied at the Metropolitan School of Art and quickly made her mark as an artist, but marriage and four children may have been partly responsible for the fact that she more or less dropped out of public view for twenty years. Resuming her career in the 1960s, she gradually rebuilt her reputation, which climaxed in a retrospective exhibition at the RHA Gallagher Gallery in 1999. Her work consists mainly of small bronzes, modelled with exceptional subtlety. Member of Aosdána and an HRHA.

LOWNDES, Alan (1921-1978) – English painter, born in Stockport, Cheshire. Served as a private through WW II. Largely self-thought, Lowndes painted full-time from 1948 and moved to Cornwall in 1959, but spent his last years in Gloucestershire. Many of his pictures dealt with the industrial and working-class milieu in which he grew up, but his palette was clear and colourful rather than sombre. Though rather an outsider and dissident among abstract painters, Lowndes was represented in the heavyweight exhibition *St Ives 1939-1964*, mounted at the Tate Gallery London in 1985.

McSWEENEY, Seán (1935-) – Irish painter, born in Dublin, but known mainly for his interpretation of the Irish landscape. For years he lived with his family in Co Wicklow, but later moved to his mother's birthplace, Ballyconnell in Co Sligo. Here he has painted, almost obsessively, an area of bog close to his studio-home, as well as the nearby Atlantic and the woods around Lissadell. Exhibits regularly at the Taylor Galleries in Dublin, and his work has been seen in the UK, US, France, Switzerland, Australia and Brussels. Retrospective exhibition mounted for Galway Arts Week in 1990, travelling to the RHA Gallagher Gallery in Dublin. Member of Aosdána and an HRHA.

MITCHELL, Denis (1912-1993) – English sculptor, born in Middlesex but spending much of his youth in Swansea. In Cornwall he worked as a miner and fisherman to earn a living, and for ten years as an assistant to Barbara Hepworth in her St Ives studio. His own work shows the imprint of her style, but it possesses a rugged integrity and strength of its own, backed by fine craftsmanship. Later he moved to Newlyn. Mitchell's innate decency and solid good sense made him a much-respected personality in Cornish art circles.

NICHOLSON, Ben (1894-1982) – English painter, a pioneer of Modernism in Britain and among its key figures from the 1920s onwards. Born in Buckinghamshire, he studied at the Slade and established strong links with Modernist groups on the Continent, absorbing the lessons of both Cubism and abstraction. His incisive intelligence, energetic work habits and technical perfectionism became models for many younger artists. Nicholson settled in St Ives in 1939 with Barbara Hepworth, his second wife. His first wife had been the gifted painter Winifred Roberts. He moved to Switzerland on his third marriage, to Felicitas Vogler, later returning to England. Nicholson established a world reputation and was awarded the OM in 1968.

O'CASEY, Breon (1928-) – born in London, son of the playwright Seán O'Casey, he attended Dartington Hall and later studied painting at the Anglo-French Art Centre in London. Moved to St Ives in the late 1950s. To support himself and his young family he worked for a time as a studio assistant to Barbara Hepworth. He turned to jewellery and weaving, winning a reputation in both fields, and more recently has branched out successfully as a sculptor, but his original vocation as a painter has reasserted itself strongly in the past two decades. Also a printmaker, O'Casey now lives and works near Penzance.

O'MALLEY, Tony (1913-) – Irish painter, born in Callan, Co Kilkenny. He worked for years as a bank official, painting almost in secret and rarely exhibiting his work. Visits to St Ives in the 1950s, originally to work in St Peter's Loft, led him to settle there in 1960 where he became friendly with Lanyon, Hilton, Bryan Wynter, Nancy Wynne-Jones, etc. Belated discovery of him in his homeland led to a retrospective exhibition in Belfast, Dublin and Cork, and in 1990 he returned to his native place, Callan, with his Canadian artist-wife Jane (née Harris, b.1944). O'Malley has since received various official honours, including the rank of Saoí in Aosdána.

PEARCE, Colman (1938-) – Irish musician, born in Dublin. Studied the violin and piano, winning prizes as a pianist before taking a degree in music at the National University of Ireland. Began conducting in his late teens, and studied in Hilversum and Vienna. Principal conductor of the RTÉ Symphony Orchestra (1981-83), principal guest conductor of the Bilbao Symphony Orchestra (1984-87), and from 1987 to 1999 he was music director and principal conductor of the Mississippi Symphony Orchestra. A noted exponent of contemporary music, , his own compositions have been performed on RTÉ and in the US.

PENDER, Jack (1918-1998) – English painter, born in Mousehole, the descendant of a line of Cornish fishing and seafaring folk. Studied art in Penzance, but was soon caught up in WW II and served as an infantryman. Resumed painting after that time, and also taught in Plymouth and Dartmouth. Elected Bard of the Cornish Gorsedd in 1965. His pictures were often of fishing boats, sailor men and harbour scenes, painted in a tonality which emphasised black and white.

SKEAPING, John (1901-1980) – English sculptor, born in Essex, best known for his animal subjects. He trained at Blackheath School of Art, Goldsmiths' College, and the RA Schools. In 1925 he married the sculptor Barbara Hepworth, by whom he had a son, but they parted after six years. Married again in 1934, to Morwenna Ward, and during WW II served in army Intelligence and the SAS. Later he taught at the RCA. Skeaping's work of the 1920s and '30s showed great style and originality, but his later sculptures were relatively academic and conventional.

SOUTER, Camille (1929-) – painter, born in Northampton, but closely identified with Irish art since the 1950s. She lived and worked for a time in Italy, painting at first in an abstract, quasi-Tachiste manner, but gradually moved into a figurative and intimist style influenced by Bonnard. For many years she lived in Co Wicklow, but has since moved to Achill in Co Mayo. Her second husband, Frank Morris, was a gifted but short-lived sculptor. Her work tends to be small, tonally subtle, and allusive, and she has added to her subject matter the impressions garnered from flying a small plane. Retrospective at the Model Arts Centre in Sligo in 2001, which travelled to the RHA Gallagher Gallery in Dublin. Member of Aosdána and an HRHA.

STUART, Imogen (1927-) – German-born sculptor domiciled in Ireland, where she has lived and worked for half a century. Born in Berlin, daughter of the writer and art critic Bruno Werner, she studied in Bavaria under the Expressionist sculptor Otto Hitzberger. In Ireland she married the sculptor Ian Stuart, with whom she had three daughters, but later separated from him. Much of her work has been for Catholic churches. Her style is influenced by Romanesque, Egyptian and Celtic art, yet retains a strong, direct personality. Member of Aosdána and Professor of Sculpture to the RHA.

TUNNARD, John (1900-1971) – major and original English painter, still somewhat underrated in spite of the advocacy of Herbert Read and others. Born in Bedfordshire, he studied at the RCA while also playing in jazz bands. Involved in textile design until he decided to paint full-time, about the time of his discovery of Cornwall in 1930. He and his wife moved there a few years later. His style has strong elements of Surrealist fantasy, though with a basis in nature and the sea. Tunnard was sometimes labelled as being part of the 'New Romanticism' of the 1940s, but his work is *sui generis*.

WAKEFORD, Edward (1914-1973) – English painter, born in the Isle of Man, son of a vicar and a half-Polish mother. He studied at Chelsea Art College and the RCA, and served in WW II. Later he taught at Chelsea and exhibited in some of the premier galleries in London (Marlborough, Leicester, etc), and his work was acquired by the Tate Gallery and others. Elected ARA in 1965, and in 1971 won the Edward Austin Abbey Award. Painted both city scenes and landscapes in a realist but highly personal style. Wakeford's autobiographical *A Prize for Art* was published by Macmillan in 1961. He also published articles, stories and poems.

WALLIS, Alfred (1855-1942) – retired sailor turned painter, whose status as one of the founding fathers of St Ives art has become almost legendary. He took up painting in old age after his wife's death, and was discovered in the 1920s by Ben Nicholson and Christopher Wood. Little known except to a minority of artists and admirers, but his quasi-primitive style was enormously influential, not only on Nicholson and Wood themselves, and on Lanyon's early work, but on painters outside St Ives such as David Jones and Winifred Nicholson.

WEJCHERT, Alexandra (1921-95) – Polish abstract sculptor and painter, born in Cracow and trained in Warsaw, where she studied architecture as well as art. During WW II she lost many friends and witnessed harrowing sights. In the 1960s she defected abroad with her small son, eventually settling in Ireland. Though her early creations were mainly paintings and reliefs, increasingly she turned to sculpture in steel and perspex, using forms which were rhythmic and organic rather than angular. Carried out some major commissions, including the great two-pronged steel sculpture outside the AIB Bank complex in Ballsbridge, Dublin.

WELLS, John (1907-2000) – born in London, he first studied medicine but also attended art classes at St Martin's School. Practiced as a doctor in the Scilly Isles from 1936 to 1945, and painted part-time until he left medicine for art. Friendly with Nicholson, Hepworth and Naum Gabo. For many years he shared a studio in Newlyn with Denis Mitchell. His style has elements of Constructivism, and also shows the influence of both Nicholson and Lanyon, but Wells was an important and individual artist in his own right. A retrospective exhibition was mounted at the Tate Gallery St Ives shortly before his death.

WESCHKE, Karl (1925-) – German-born painter from Thuringia, active in Cornwall from 1955 onwards. Conscripted into the Luftwaffe while still in his teens, he was captured in Holland and came to Britain as a prisoner of war. Studied at St Martin's School in London in the late 1940s, later moving to Cornwall. Weschke was friendly with most of the St Ives artists, and exhibited at the Penwith and in other group shows, but his figurative, quasi-Expressionist style rather set him apart from the local abstractionists.

WYNTER, Bryan (1915-1975) – English painter of the St Ives School, whose work evolved out of a kind of neo-Romantic, slightly Surreal style into his own brand of 'informal' abstraction. Born in London, he studied at the Slade, and during WW II he worked on the land as a conscientious objector, as did his friend Patrick Heron. Wynter moved to Cornwall in 1945 and later taught in Corsham for several years. During the 1960s he created some striking Kinetic works, which were reassembled in the Tate Gallery St Ives long after his death. A memorial exhibition was mounted at the Hayward Gallery in London in 1976.

Drawings

Ludgvan
1958, conté on paper, 38 × 51 cm (15 × 20 in)

Trevalgan
1963, crayon on paper, 38 × 51 cm (15 × 20 in)

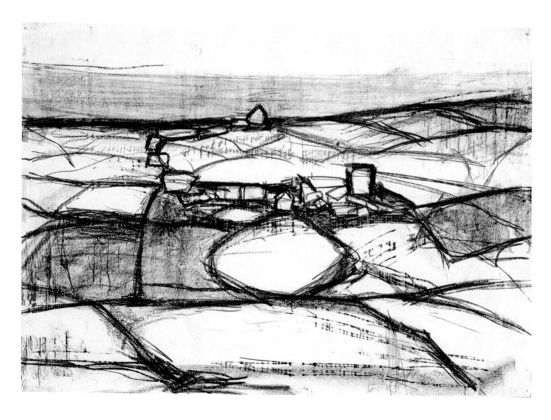

Rosemergy
1965, conté on paper, 18 × 25.5 cm (7 × 10 in)

Cornish Landscape
1959, conté on paper, 38 × 51 cm (15 × 20 in)

John
1974, conté on paper, 25.5 × 35 cm (10 × 13.75 in)

Bridget
1977, pencil, 29 × 42 cm (11.5 × 16.5 in), detail

John and Bridget Drawing
1973, ink and crayon on paper, 21.5 × 30 cm (8.5 × 11.75 in)

Rose Farm
1982, oil pastel on paper; 30 × 41 cm (11.75 × 16.25 in)

The Farm on the Hill
1982, oil pastel on paper; 30 × 41 cm (11.75 × 16.25 in)

Cornish Field
1966, oil pastel on paper, 24 × 32 cm (9.5 × 12.5 in)

Clonmacnoise
1966, oil pastel on paper, 25.5 × 35 cm (10 × 13.75 in)

Eucalyptus plant
'75

Interior with Landscape, Kinsale
1977, conté on paper, 30 × 23 cm (11.75 × 9 in)

Eucalyptus Plant
1975, ink on paper, 21 × 30 cm (8.25 × 11.75 in)

Still Life
1973, sepia ink on paper, 21.5 × 32 cm (8.5 × 12.5 in)

View Near St Remy
1966, oil pastel on paper, 20 × 27 cm (8 × 10.75 in)

Mons Guinec's Barn
1989, water pastel on paper, 30 × 41 cm (11.75 × 16.25 in)

Picasso's Vauvenargues
1979, oil pastel on paper, 28 × 38 cm (11 × 15 in)

Cézanne's Studio at Aix
1979, oil pastel on paper, 28 × 38 cm (11 × 15 in)

Ballycastle Bay
1996, mixed media, 30 x 41 cm (11.75 x 16.25 in)

Shed with Trees
1996, mixed media, 30 × 41 cm (11.75 × 16.25 in)

Road with Pale Grass
2001, oil pastel on paper, 30 x 41 cm (11.75 x 16.25 in)

Bellacorick Bog with Corslieve
2001, oil pastel on paper, 30 x 41 cm (11.75 x 16.25 in)

Bog with Nephin
2001, oil pastel on paper; 30 × 41 cm (11.75 × 16.25 in)

The Top of the Road
2000, oil pastel on paper; 30 × 41 cm (11.75 × 16.25 in)

Artist's Notebook

NANCY WYNNE-JONES

A NOTE ON PETER LANYON'S TEACHING AT ST PETER'S LOFT

First of all, he didn't really teach as such. I don't ever remember him telling anyone what to do or what not to do, except in the case of purely technical things such as grinding colours or mixing size. What he tried to do in the Loft, I think, was to make us aware that we tended to see the world through unquestioned visual conventions, and, on the whole, painted it by equally unquestioned artistic rules. To see freshly, to paint using only your own will in concept and method – to do what you wanted, and at the same time be aware of all that's gone before – that's what he wanted to give us the courage to do.

Not everybody liked it in the very mixed lot of people who came and went to and from the Loft. Although they were all charmed by Peter, some of them preferred to be taught by Bill Redgrave. I remember one woman, a nice, middle-aged amateur, saying to me as she tried despairingly to paint a vase of sweet william (of all things!): 'Why doesn't Peter tell me how to do it?'

He wouldn't do that, but he would sometimes point one in the direction of the Old Masters and suggest that one looked to see how they tackled similar problems. There were a number of art books in the Loft for us to browse in – Delacroix's journals, Herbert Read's *Art Now* (known to Peter as 'Art Then'). We could discuss any new art book, poetry too, in exemplifying the creative principle at work.

His teaching at the Loft was mostly landscape-oriented, and he would take us out to places like Botallack to experience the sea and land with our bodies as well as our eyes. But quite often there was also a model for those more interested in the figurative, and I remember a lively discussion on Matisse's nudes and semi-nudes. Also, Peter would set out still lifes of incredible beauty around the walls, on little tables. I remember one in particular, all varying shades of green, which I tried to paint and gave up in a rage, because I couldn't make a painting as beautiful as the original.

Peter would reiterate the necessity of continually drawing. We tried drawing in one continuous line, just letting our eyes move about the room, picking up whatever interested us. A cross between Matisse and Tobey. Very interesting spatially. We also did some exercises in Gabo's spiral space, and some glass sculpture, using pieces of glass found on the beach. Mostly, however, we did our own thing, using Peter's strength and courage to help us break through our hesitations and cowardices.

(c.1993)

THOUGHTS ON PAINTING LANDSCAPE

The poet WS Graham has said: 'What do I weep and lack other / Than all that is not me?', and the landscape, whether we see it out of a window while safely in our houses, or whether we are walking about in it and feeling it all around us, is essentially not us. It is irredeemably other. I believe it is this desire of artists to possess this other, to get into a relationship with it, that makes us paint the landscape.

Monet wanted to possess a landscape halted forever at a particular moment in time, exactly as it was. He said somewhere, I think, that he tried to see it as if he had never seen it before, as if he didn't know what leaves were, or trees, or water, but painted only what his eye saw. Whoever it was that said – wasn't it Cézanne? – Monet was 'only an eye, but what an eye' missed the point. To be just an eye was exactly what Monet wanted to be, and it is a very hard thing to do, to separate what you see from what you know. (After all, Giacometti spent his whole life trying to do just that, but that's another story.)

Bonnard is interesting on this. He used to go for walks every morning with his dog Poucette, and he carried with him a tiny sketchbook and a pencil, and when he saw something that interested him he made a drawing of it immediately and came home and painted it – a painting that might take him months or even years to complete. He didn't elaborate the drawing, and he didn't paint on the spot, because he said that only in your first glance do you see what really interests you, and you see it as a whole, everything in the correct relations. If you looked longer you saw other things, and you put them in as well, and the relations got confused and the immediacy was lost.

Of course not everybody wants immediacy. Memory of what we have known about a place is an important part of painting for some artists. Primitives like James Dixon and Alfred Wallis paint places and things as they know them to be, not as they see them at a particular time, a particular place. A harbour is round, and is surrounded by houses, which are seen from the front because that is how they know them to be. They will paint a rowboat from above, because they remember how it looks when they get into it, but a sailing ship will be seen from the side because they remember seeing it like that from the sea – which they usually paint very well, incidentally. Sometimes they put in their dreams. Alfred Wallis painted ships among icebergs, and sometimes with fish swimming under the keel – 'the souls of sailors', he said.

Wallis lived in St Ives and only started painting when he was over 70 – 'for company', as he said, after his wife died. He greatly influenced Ben Nicholson, his example helping Nicholson to break away from a perspective-based construction of landscape. This was a different way of dealing with space. Instead of having your picture a deep hole, everything was brought – unconsciously in the case of Wallis, consciously in the case of Nicholson – into relation with the picture surface, a more conceptual device than perspective, perhaps, but then western perspective is also a device, just one way of conveying spatial depth. Bernard Leach, the great English potter, who lived so many years in Japan, told me once that he took a Japanese artist around the Alte Pinakothek in Munich, which was full of marvellous Old Master drawings. They looked and looked, and at the end the Japanese said yes, it was very interesting, but why were all western artists so mannered? It made them hard to understand.

Classical Chinese and Japanese perspective is, I believe, the opposite of ours – the vanishing point is behind your head, and the world fans out before you, and I must say that seems to make a lot of sense too. I suppose aerial perspective, the fact that near things look big and far things small, has to be common to us all, but even that is a thing that isn't naturally understood by us; we have to learn it in infancy by memory and experience. How we see is as much mental as it is visual, and there are all kinds of ways of making visible our understanding of the world.

The great Russian Constructivist Gabo watched the big Atlantic waves rolling in to the beach in St Ives, and concluded, from watching them arch and turn, that all space was spiral. His sculptures demonstrated this with great beauty. But they are images, diagrams almost, of pure space. You can't touch grass or feel rain in them. His pupil Peter Lanyon developed a way of using this spiral space to include the weather and the feel and the weight of the land, as well as its rhythms. He was passionately attached to the western end of Cornwall called West Penwith, where he was born, and he forged a very original way of expressing his understanding of it. Taking the Cubist multiple viewpoint, and attaching it to Gabo's interpretation of space as spiral, he painted pictures which took whole areas of country, and compacted them into images in which whirled the thinness of cliffs as he climbed them, the softness of grass as he looked through it, the colour of a beach in the evening, the movement of the sea, the shape of the harbour, the sadness of the history of a place where tin had been mined for centuries and many men had died in mine disasters – a big, complex amalgam which was sometimes confused but always evocative of reality, because of its honesty to his own experience.

Peter was my teacher, and I knew him well. I remember one time he'd been staying in Derbyshire and came back very excited because he had seen that the stone walls of Derbyshire looked white between the fields. 'At last I can put white lines in my painting,' he said. He said several other things which are interesting about landscape. One day he showed me a seagull flying between the cliff we were on and a more distant one, and pointed out how his flight articulated the space. Another time we were looking at a big brown net spread out to dry on the grass on the Island at St Ives, and he said: 'We know the net is on top of the grass, but visually it's a dark hole in the green.' He told me the pale ochre fuzz in one of his paintings (that was *Rosewall*, which is now in the Ulster Museum) was out-of-focus summer grass as you saw it when lying down and looking through it.

Close-up landscape can be, has to be, very tactile. You are hit by the subject matter, especially if the painting is big. Did any of you see the big Bonnard exhibition in London? In it there were some marvellous paintings of his garden. From across the room you saw bushes and trees and flowers; if you went close these dissolved into many-coloured marks; if you went right up to them and put your head really close to them, it was exactly as if you were walking in that garden – twigs were scratching your face and leaves were moving in the corner of your eye.

Monet, of course, brought you close to the waters of his pond. I have tried to bring you close to my pond in some of my paintings. There is an intimacy about paintings of gardens or ponds. Ivon Hitchens has it in his woodland paintings, Seán McSweeney has it in his paintings of his bog, with its little pools that reflect the sky and its brilliant bog flowers. And here too is the transforming eye. No doubt we would find Hitchens's wood a dullish place; I've seen Seán's bog and found it ordinary enough, but how beautiful the paintings. The mind and the eye. Beckmann said we should never get too far from the eye or we became silly, but the mind comes into it, and especially love for the place we paint. It may be love for a place we know well, it may be the excitement of falling in love with a new place. Matisse and Derain, in Collioure, had to develop a new way of painting – Fauvism – to express their delight in discovering Mediterranean light. Because Jack Yeats knew the west of Ireland so well, he knew what is magical about it – that the light penetrates everything, and that the spaces are wide and filled with the colours of the air. Air is coloured everywhere but it is especially so in the west, and the whole of a late Yeats painting, land and air, is filled with flecks and stabs of coloured light.

There is a transparency about these late landscapes. Nothing is solid, the air is as full of colour as the land, it is all alive and vibrating. Figures – people, horses – appear and disappear. I am told that he always painted the landscape first and that people and horses walked into it as he painted, without his volition. It happened to him in life as well. He told Gerard Shanahan, the pianist and collector of Yeats, that one summer evening he was walking across a field in Sligo, and in a corner of the field was a girl having a bath in a horse trough. He put this mythic scene into a painting – the Rococo ceiling of the theatre in the picture called *Now!*.

But it is his light that is most interesting, his handling of, solidifying almost, of the air in-between. In any wide landscape, especially a flattish one such as a wide bogland, there is a large amount of undefined nothing between you and the distance. Yeats filled up this nothing with coloured light and air, building up a space as wide and as alive as one feels space to be, sky and land melting into each other. Perhaps one feels this most in the bigger paintings. With a big painting, any big painting, you can't see all of it unless you are very far away from it, and the movement of your eye as it travels over the picture surface increases your feeling of being in it. It becomes environmental. The huge American Abstract Expressionist paintings weren't meant to be seen from a distance, as they are usually hung in galleries. They were intended for the walls of small New York apartments, where they loomed over the furniture and became a moving, energetic part of the room. Jack Yeats' paintings give the same feeling of living space.

Wide space and the air in-between is something which interests me very much. I have attempted in some of my paintings to animate the space between my eye and the further reaches of my landscape with a variety of metaphors for the air in-between. I feel that you do not see the air as empty. It seems alive and full of incident, it is coloured in itself, and also your eye picks up and transfers colours from the land and sky. In sunlight the colour yellow comes into everything – think of van Gogh. It all moves and quivers, sometimes almost in pillars of air, sometimes in a quiet rhythm derived from the rhythm of the land, sometimes it glitters like the sea. I have tried to make metaphors for these things, to paint pictures which are like being in the landscape rather than just looking at the landscape.

(excerpt from lecture by the artist at Douglas Hyde Gallery, Dublin, 5 April 1995)

———

MY DISCOVERY OF MAYO

Going to Mayo on a Ballinglen fellowship in 1994 was a turning-point in my life and in my work. It immediately excited me. The landscape wasn't like any I had seen before. I would wake up at five in the morning to see the morning mist slowly clear from the huge green landscape. I became delightedly aware of the immensity of the space around me, and the urge grew somehow to possess it in my work.

I found the pace of life in Mayo was slow. People had time to talk to you, you had time to think and absorb the feel of the land. The sacred mountain appeared and disappeared. I found the bogs.

On that first visit I tried out new ways of treating space, combining traditional perspective with on-the-surface forms. Not very satisfactory, but at least a way of combining two ways of treating space, two ways I had always kept separate before.

In subsequent visits, inland Mayo became more important to me than the coast. We began staying in Enniscoe House. Conor fished on Lough Conn or Carramore, I drove out to Bellacorick and drew the great Maumkeogh Bog over and over again. Eventually we rented a cottage in the stableyard of Enniscoe. So now when we go to Mayo, we go from one home to another. In Enniscoe I wake up to see Nephin outside my bedroom window. Sometimes there is a hare stepping curiously out of the wood. Nearly always there is a blackbird.

Out on the big bog, the feeling of space is amazing. It feels like the beginning of the world, before man was thought of, both awe-inspiring and energising. The marks of old turf-cuttings articulate the bog, the air is filled with light bouncing back from the mountains, contradicting the big receding distance. The mountains are both near and far, the multi-coloured bog both solid and ephemeral.

I had to evolve a way of making something which could begin to convey the complexity of this huge, simple landscape. So I began to try to make my strokes and stabs and smudges of paint themselves fill the space between the mountains and my possessing eye. My categories of space – traditional, shallow – became irrelevant. Here I had to do something new.

The Maumkeogh Bog is many-coloured, multi-textured, with its orange moss, its small dull-green bushes, its heather and glaze of purple grasses. Sometimes the whole stretch seems fiery. The mountains are blue or grey, sharply horizoned or half-hidden in cloud. Corslieve has a cairn on the high point, erected to who knows what king or hero. Nephin looms quietly above Lough Conn.

I feel that working here I am combining all my earlier approaches, and am at last painting the landscape in a way which has evolved from it, a way that has grown naturally from the great Mayo spaces.

(2002)

———

List of Art Illustrations

———

DRAWINGS

Nancy Wynne-Jones

A CHRONOLOGY

1922 • Born 10 December at Penmaenucha, Dolgellau, Merioneth, North Wales to Charles Llewellyn Wynne-Jones and Sybil Mary Gella (née Scott). The youngest of three children, having two brothers, Charles Alexander (Alec), born 1917, and Ronald (Polly), born 1919. Educated entirely at home because of ill-health.

1932 • Drawing classes in Sherborne, Dorset, where the family spent a large part of every year in nearby Thornhill, Stalbridge. Taught by Mrs Gervis, a children's book illustrator.
• Encouraged in her interest in poetry, painting and music by JR Heath, the family's doctor, who had a wide interest in the arts. A composer, he conducted his own works with the Halle Orchestra and at Promenade Concerts in London.

1936 • Read Herbert Read's book *Art Now*, which came as a revelation

1938 • Began studying the violin and composing music

1940 • Entered the Royal Academy of Music, London, to study violin and composition

1941 • Death of eldest brother, Alec, in action in north Africa

1942 • Death of second brother, Polly, in action in north Africa

1943 • Left Royal Academy of Music and volunteered to do war work at the Ordnance Survey

1945 • Left the Ordnance Survey soon after the end of the war, and worked in bookshops for experience, with a view to opening her own bookshop

1946 • Bought the Forum Bookshop in Fulham

1950 • Sold bookshop

1951 • Entered Heatherley's, an atelier-type art school in London

1955 • Left Chelsea on retirement of Edward Wakeford and painted on her own

1957 • Went to St Ives, Cornwall, to study with Peter Lanyon
• First paintings to be seen in public shown at the Pasmore Edwards Gallery in Newlyn (now the Newlyn Gallery), and exhibited there regularly until 1972

1958 • Lived and worked alone in the Battery, on the Island at St Ives, with the encouragement of Lanyon

1959 • Included in *Eleven British Artists*, Jefferson Place Gallery, Washington DC, with Lanyon, Hilton, Heron, etc

1960 • *20 Cornish Painters*, Polytechnic Gallery, Falmouth, with Lanyon, Hilton, etc

1962 • Bought 'Trevaylor', a country house near Gulval, Penzance, and moved there to live
• First one-person show in New Vision Centre, London
• Painting *Lazarus* bought by the Arts Council of Great Britain
• Included in *The Arts Council as Patron*, Arts Council Gallery, London.
• ICA Picture Fair, London, with Gillian Ayres, William Gear, etc

1963 • One-person exhibition in Galleria Numero, Florence
• Exhibited at *Mostra Internationazale d'Arte d'Avantguardia*, Livorno
• *Pictures for Schools*, Midland Group Gallery, Nottingham
• London Galleries, Leeds
• Midland 21, Nottingham
• Commonwealth Biennale of Abstract Art, London
• *Kunstenaars Uit Newlyn*, Kultural Centrum, Ostend

1964 • One-person exhibition in Dolgellau, Wales
• NVC Artists, Galerie Wirth, Berlin

1967 • Moved back into Trevaylor

1970 • Adopted John and Bridget, brother and sister, aged three and one
   • One-person exhibition, Project Arts Centre, Abbey Street, Dublin – first show in Ireland

1972 • Moved to Scilly House, Kinsale, Co Cork

1974 • Death of father and father-in-law, the poet Padraic Fallon

1975 • Death of mother
   • One-person show, Emmet Gallery, Dublin

1977 • Joint exhibition with Conor Fallon, Emmet Gallery, Dublin

1978 • Joint exhibition with Conor Fallon, Lad Lane Gallery, Dublin

1980 • *The Probity of Art*, Oriel Gallery, Cardiff

1981 • *The Shadow of My Hand*, Oriel Gallery, Cardiff
   • *La Integridad del Arte*, Centro Cultural de la Ville de Madrid
   • Lincoln Gallery, Dublin

1982 • One-person show, Lincoln Gallery, Dublin

1985 • *Cork Art Now*, Crawford Municipal Art Gallery, Cork, and Amsterdam
   • One-person exhibition, Lincoln Gallery, Dublin

1986 • Figurative Image, Bank of Ireland, Dublin

1987 • Moved to Rathdrum, Co Wicklow
   • Figurative Image, Bank of Ireland, Dublin

1988 • Hendriks Gallery International, New York
   • One-person show, Hendriks Gallery, Dublin
   • Figurative Image, Royal Hospital, Dublin
   • *Celtic Vision*, Bank of Ireland, Dublin

1989 • Oireachtas Art Exhibition, RHA Gallagher Gallery, Dublin

1991 • One-person exhibition, Carroll Gallery, Longford
   • Included in *Great Book of Ireland*

1992 • Retrospective exhibition, University College Cork, touring to Galway Arts Centre; Limerick City Gallery of Art; Glebe Gallery, Co Donegal; RHA Gallagher Gallery, Dublin
   • *Art Lovers*, Boathouse Gallery, Castletownshend, Co Cork
   • *British Abstract Art of the Fifties and Sixties*, Belgrave Gallery, London

1993 • Boyle Arts Festival, group exhibition
   • *Couples*, Boathouse Gallery, Castletownshend, Co Cork
   • Ferguson Collection, RHA Gallagher Gallery, Dublin

1994 • Elected honorary member of the Royal Hibernian Academy
   • Awarded fellowship by Ballinglen Arts Foundation; first work in Mayo
   • Art Alliance, Philadelphia

1995 • One-person exhibition, Taylor Galleries, Dublin

1996 • Elected member of Aosdána
   • Éigse Carlow Arts Festival

1997 • *The Poetry of Place*, one-person exhibition, Taylor Galleries, Dublin

1998 • Visited South Africa
   • *AIB Art on Tour*, touring Ireland

1999 • Anthony Cronin Tribute Exhibition, Claremorris, Co Mayo
   • *Tony O'Malley Selects*, Lavit Gallery, Cork

2000 • *Here and Africa*, one-person exhibition, Taylor Galleries, Dublin
   • *Artists' Century*, RHA Gallagher Gallery, Dublin
   • *Basil Blackshaw and Friends*, Boyle Arts Festival

d Friends, Boyle Arts

BIBLIOGRAPHY

(Most entries denote exhibition reviews unless otherwise stated)

1962 • Christopher Salvesen, *Arts Review*, 10 Feb
• Christopher Salvesen, *Arts Review*, 20 April
• Myfanwy Kitchen, *Guardian*, 27 March
• Martin J Kemp, *Arts Review*, 3 April

1970 • Terry O'Sullivan, *Evening Press*, Dublin, 18 Feb
• Diarmuid Peavoy, *Evening Herald*, March
• Bruce Arnold, *Irish Independent*, March
• Brian Fallon, *Irish Times*, 23 Feb
• unsigned, *Irish Times*, 17 Feb
• unsigned, *Irish Press*, 18 Feb

1975 • Patrick Glendon, *Irish Independent*, May
• unsigned, *Irish Times*, 8 May
• Una Lehane, interview with the artist, *Irish Times*, May

1977 • Harriet Cooke, *Irish Times*, 16 Feb
• Patrick Glendon, *Irish Independent*, Feb
• PF Byrne, *Evening Herald*, 15 Feb

1978 • Ciarán MacGonigal, *Irish Times*, 7 Sept

1979 • *The Arts Council of Great Britain Collection* (hardback catalogue)

1980 • Adrian Heath, introduction to catalogue *The Probity of Art* (Welsh Arts Council, Cardiff)

1981 • Spanish edition of above
• Artist's statement in catalogue *The Shadow of My Hand* (Welsh Arts Council, Cardiff)
• Hilary Pyle, *Irish Times*, 12 February

1982 • Patrick Glendon, *Irish Independent*, 15 May
• Desmond MacAvock, Irish Times, 7 May
• Bliathín Ní Ciobhain, *Irish Press*, 7 May

1984 • Aidan Dunne, *Sunday Press*, 22 April

1985 • Aidan Dunne, introduction to catalogue for one-person exhibition, Lincoln Gallery, Dublin
• Aidan Dunne, *Sunday Press*, 20 Nov
• Tom O'Reilly, *Irish Times*, 19 Nov
• Vera Ryan, catalogue introduction to *Cork Art Now* (Crawford Municipal Art Gallery, Cork)

1988 • Brian Fallon, catalogue introduction for one-person exhibition, Hendriks Gallery, Dublin

1990 • Aidan Dunne, *Sunday Tribune*, 13 May
• Desmond MacAvock, *Irish Times*, 15 April

1992 • Tom O'Reilly, *Irish Times*, 3 April
• Hilary O'Kelly, introduction to catalogue of retrospective exhibition (University College Cork)
• Brian Fallon, catalogue essay for above
• Aidan Dunne, catalogue essay for above
• unsigned, *Cork Examiner*, 13 April
• Hilary Pyle, *Irish Times*, 21 April
• unsigned, *Galway Advertiser*, 28 May
• Tom O'Reilly, *Irish Times*, 11 June
• Vera Ryan, catalogue introduction for one-person exhibition, Taylor Galleries, Dublin
• Aidan Dunne, *Sunday Tribune*, 11 Nov
• Patrick Gallagher, *Sunday Independent*, 15 Nov
• Frances Ruane, *Irish Times*, 18 Nov

1993 • Brian Fallon, 'As I Was Going to St Ives', *Irish Times*, 4 Aug
• Tom O'Reilly. 'Sligo Arts Festival', *Irish Times*, 14 Sept

1994 • Brian Fallon, *Irish Times*, 13 Oct
• Brian Fallon, *Irish Art 1930-1990* (Appletree Press, Belfast)
• Peter Davies, *St Ives Revisited* (Old Bakehouse Publications, Gwent)

1995 • Brian Fallon, *Irish Times*, 28 April
• Aidan Dunne, 'Where West Meets West', *Sunday Tribune*, 9 April

1996 • Dorothy Walker, *Modern Art in Ireland* (Lilliput Press, Dublin)

1997 • Aidan Dunne, *Sunday Tribune*, 19 Oct
• Brian Fallon, *Irish Times*, 24 Oct

2000 • Catherine Daly, *Sunday Times*, 19 June
• Aidan Dunne, *Irish Times*, 6 July

2002 • Aidan Dunne, *Irish Times*, 8 May

———

Index

215